Connie's Miracles

a story of Faith

By

Cameron Hoggard Clark

This book is dedicated to

My Lord and Savior, Jesus Christ, who gave me the ability to write and for the most part, the words to write

Burns Homer Clark (my son), my miraculous gift from God, my earthly reason to wake each day with a smile; the joy of my heart

Carlton and Carol Lou Hoggard (Daddy and Momma), givers of love, patience, support, and encouragement

Homer and Myrtle Burns (Grandaddy and Grandmomma), an earthly mirror image of Christ to me

Connie Hoggard Terry ("Sweet Sister"), the reason for this story, the diamond that now shines in the Glory of our Heavenly Father

Contents

Introduction

1 Just Start 1

2 Precious Designed Favor...........................6

3 Precious Memories, Stored up Treasure.....27

4 Just Connie..34

5 Change 42

6 Just Praise...55

7 Preparations for Home 64

8 Just a Little While 71

9 Father, No!..82

10 In His Presence 91

11 All Creatures Great and Small 99

12 Faith No More 107

13 Guiding Hand...119

14 Jesus Take the Wheel, Faith Drives.........125

15 Miracles Continue 136

16 Joy Come in the 'Mourning'.....................156

17 Thank you, Lord 171

Introduction

Psalm 71

In thee, O Lord, do I put my trust; let me never be put to confusion. Deliver me in thy righteousness, and cause me to escape; incline thine ear unto me, and save me. Be thou my strong habitation, where unto I may continually resort; thou hast given commandment to save me; for thou art my rock and my fortress. Deliver me, O my God, out of the hand of the wicked, out of the hand of the unrighteous and cruel man. For thou art my hope, O Lord God; thou art my trust from my youth. By thee have I been holden up from the womb; thou art He that took me out of my mother's womb; my praise shall be continually of thee. I am as a wonder unto many; but thou art my strong refuge. Let my mouth be filled with thy praise and with thy honor all the day. Cast me not off in the time of old age; forsake me not when my strength faileth. For mine enemies speak against me; and they that lay wait for me should take counsel together. Saying, God hath forsaken him; persecute and take him; for there is none to deliver him. O God, be not far from me: O my God, make haste for my help. Let them be confounded and consumed that are adversaries to my soul; let them be covered with reproach and dishonor that seek my hurt. But I will hope continually, and will yet praise thee more and more. My mouth shall show forth thy righteousness and thy salvation all the day; for I know not the numbers thereof. I will go in the strength of the Lord God; I will make mention of thy righteousness, even of thine only. O God, thou hast taught me from my youth; and hitherto have I declared thy wondrous works. Now also when I am old and gray headed, O God, forsake me not; until I have showed thy strength unto this generation, and thy power to every one that is to come. Thy righteousness also, O God, is very high, who hast done great things: O God, who is like unto thee! Thou, which hast shown me great and sore troubles, shalt quicken me again, and shalt bring me up again from the depths of the earth. Thou shalt increase my greatness, and comfort me on every side. I will also praise thee with the psaltry, even thy truth, O my God: unto thee will I sing with the harp, O thou Holy One of Israel. My lips shall greatly rejoice when I sing unto thee; and my soul, which thou hast redeemed. My tongue also shall talk of thy righteousness all the day long: for they are confounded, for they are brought to shame, that seek my hurt.

This Psalm has a special meaning to me. I heard a pastor say recently that he believes the chapters in Psalms directly correlate with our calendar years. I thought interesting at best, albeit his opinion. I began reading and sure enough it seemed to fit in the most amazing ways. I ventured out in simple curiosity and looked up my corresponding birth-year. I realize it wasn't written just for me, but that day, this day, it resinated with me, with how I felt, what was going on in my life, had gone on... .

Chapter 1
Just Start

*C*onnie Hoggard Terry-

Seeing that name in print makes me feel so strange and with mixed, multiple emotions. Connie was the writer, not me. She had planned to write a book for years. She loved to read and collect books as well. Reading has never been my hobby, sadly. If I read, I only read the Bible. For some reason reading just puts me to sleep. Not a good comment for a school teacher to make I know nor someone "writing" this. That's why its a bit surreal that here I sit penning this story. God uses all of us when He is ready regardless if we think we're usable or capable. If God gives us a job to do then we have to try and do our best. He will work out the details. So when God laid this on my heart, I had to try. So many times God has such great plans for us, yet we are the problem; we in our flesh block His will. We look at ourselves and doubt; that is the flesh. We have to learn that God doesn't work within the flesh; He works in the supernatural. I have been a Christian for many years, over 30 to be exact. It wasn't until recently that my eyes began to be opened to the wonders that Jesus Christ intends for our lives. Miracles and wonders are available to each one of us if we believe and are open to seeing them and accepting them.

Proverbs 3:5 - "Trust in the Lord with all thine heart; and lean not unto thine own understanding." (KJV) This is a verse most of us learned as a child and take for granted since we hear it so often. When this verse became alive in me and I truly took it to heart , it changed my whole way of thinking.

Writing wasn't something I was trained in, educated for, or even planned to attempt. This project actually began simply as a healing journal for me and a listing, if you will (record keeping), of the miracles we've been privy to. Yet when God said "write", I began to find the words through His power. When God directs us to do anything out of our comfort zone or knowledge base, it has to be done and He will provide the knowledge, means, and opportunity.

Once I understood that, the words just began to flow. I had to realize that "Cameron" wasn't going to ever do justice to this story or frankly, ever write it. The events that I will convey in this book occurred because of God's power and its under His power that they can be told.

Psalm 119:18- "Open my eyes, that I may behold wonderful things from Your law." (NKJV)

The word "law" in Hebrew is "Torah" or "teaching". There are wonderful things in God's "Word"/"teaching" for us. These wonderful things are hidden gems in Scripture, if you will, that go unseen to many. They are so wonderful that when you really see them, they change you profoundly and empower holiness in you. I went through most of my adult, Christian life, blinded. I relied solely on the teaching I'd been reared on in the church and my own feeble attempt to study the Word. An attempt that only recently I found lacking. It wasn't until I truly humbled myself to the Lord, let Him mold me, asked for knowledge to be revealed from the Holy Spirit that I began seeing these truths, His Glory. I had to get on my knees and say "teach me, Father, open my eyes that I may see." Daily, I ask for a "fresh dose of wisdom". Without this, we can not see God's total plan for us; for it is supernatural. To see the supernatural, we have to obtain the ability to live in the supernatural. We're in this world, not of this world (1 John

3

17:14-16, John 15:19). True, when we are born again we enter into a new life (2 Corinthians 5:17), but we must ask for illumination.

As I mentioned, Connie had always planned to write a book. She had started many times, but it never came to fruition. I hope in some way this will honor her desire. *Writing* the story, is a role/task she never accomplished- *being* the story, is her role now.

> Psalm 27:14- "Wait on the Lord: be of good courage, and He shall strengthen thy heart: wait, I say, on the Lord." (KJV)

> For some reason, it was not intended for Connie to write her book. Sometimes God just wants us to wait and yes, sometimes, we by our own fault, miss out on something He wanted to give.

With God's guidance, I trust I can convey a bit about Connie and the miraculous events associated with her. Its hard to know where to begin. To begin when Connie was born would be a logical starting point, but I feel that is a story for another time. I will begin as close to the beginning as I'm led. I'll ask you to forgive in advance because its most likely I may skip around a bit time-wise and possibly have a tendency to take a rabbit trail here and there and perhaps "convey" (for lack of a stronger word) my opinions. You'll probably find as well a bit of Scripture sprinkled here and there. It would be hard to tell a story that God provided and leave His Word out of it. If I give a personal opinion, I will try to back it up with Scripture.

Chapter 2
Precious Designed Favor

Connie has been my sister my whole life. I've never known life without her since I'm the younger. There were just two of us, we are a very small family, not many extended even. I'm not sure if it makes a difference or not mentioning the size. Each member of my family and yours I imagine is loved regardless of what "number" you happen to be or the size thereof.

I can't begin Connie's miraculous story without sharing a bit about our background. For I feel, these miracles were "earned" if you will many years ago and stored up for us through the Godly patriarchs/matriarchs of our family.

Our grandparents and parents weren't perfect, no human is but they sure came/come close.

We grew up in a small town where my grandparents, Homer and Myrtle Burns ("Grandmomma" and "Grandaddy") lived very close. We ate most of our meals there versus our own home. We were there a great deal. Sometimes I wondered which home was really mine. They worshipped and loved the Lord, but let me say- in the earthly realm (not to be blasphemous in any way) they worshipped me and Connie. To them, we hung the moon. We were their "world". I hope to goodness they knew the feeling was mutual!

When you are young, you take so much for granted and although you feel a certain way, you don't voice it enough. That is something I try so hard to convey to my son now.

Grandaddy & Grandmomma

Our parents were of the same mindset. To them, Connie and I were/are their world. They weren't the kind that planned things and had to make alternate plans for us. They never, not once hired a baby sitter for us. If we couldn't go, they didn't want to go. We thought this was normal, a babysitter was something only children in New York City must of had or children on TV shows. Some of you reading this may take offense to that or think I'm judgmental of parents who do things without their children. Of course not. Everyone is different and everyone does things as they see fit or as they see works best for their family or at least I hope so. You must admit though, there are tons that put their children absolutely last and look upon them as a bother/ inconvenience rather than a blessing. That's a whole other book in itself, right? Gracious! I would imagine though my thoughts on that subject would never get to their ears. Then there are some parents that need that away time to regroup/rest and be better parents for it

as do their children. I hope I explained that and when I explained
our family, that was just what worked with us.

We like all have/had problems, burdens, hurts, joys, and victories, all
of which were shared equally as one. We were small in number, but at
least for me as a child living in it, felt giant-sized as a unit.

Deuteronomy 6:7 - "And thou shalt teach them
(the laws and ways of God) diligently unto thy
children, and shalt talk of them when thou sit in thine
house, and when thou walkest by the way, and when
thou sit down, and when thou risest up." (KJV)

Explaining the relationship we had with our grandparents is another
story all on its own; although, one I'd love to share. They were such
unusual people. They loved the Lord, stood firm for morality, and
loved each other unconditionally. They were a perfect picture of how
a husband and wife should be.

They loved us immensely. Their world revolved around us as I
mentioned. I can remember, just to name one thing, if they went to
"town" (if you are from the country, that term will make sense to you)
while Connie and I were at school, they wouldn't stop to eat lunch in
town since we couldn't so they would go on home. That's just one
tiny story among thousands. As I sit here my mind is flooded with
great memories of my childhood that I would just love to take time
and share. To mention just a few, none of which are earth shattering
or perhaps noteworthy, but to me they are finer than diamonds. Tiny

8

memories of hearing Grandmomma sing out her "Yoo-Hoo!" when we would come in asking for her, hearing her sing as she cooked or took the clothes off the line, feeling her rub our backs, her cutting our food up in tiny little pieces long after we needed that help, having her cook me (just for me) a lumberjack "man" breakfast complete with coffee at the wee age of 4,5,6... only to have me eat a tiny bit compared to what was on the plate- simply because I saw it on a western and wanted to be like that cowboy, hearing her pray for us and wondering "why that made her so sad." Little did I understand then those weren't tears of sadness. Oh the mighty prayers she had with that gentle voice. To laugh at her trying to play basketball with Connie, oh how she struggled and oh how we'd laugh and her as well. To see Grandaddy looking on as he worked in his shop in the carport and laughing too. Grandaddy letting me wash the truck with a broom no less, just because I thought it would work. Grandaddy letting Connie drive to the store in the truck on the highway at the ripe old age of 6!!!

They gave to us all the time and especially at gift-giving holidays. For some reason though, Valentine's Day sticks out in my mind more than the rest, more than Christmas even. Grandaddy would buy us a big heart shaped box of candy. If it was a school day, he would almost drive Momma crazy asking "if it was time for the babies to come" yet. He was so excited to give us that candy. Other holidays more money was spent; but to me, seeing that sweet giant of a man glow this day holding that box down to me was a vision I'll never forget. I told my husband that and he never failed to make sure a big heart shaped box of candy he had for me and would always say, "from your Grandaddy" (*thank you for that, Monty*).

Grandmomma and Grandaddy were extremely intelligent in the secular (special and unusual considering the lack of formal education they had), but more importantly they knew and studied the Bible.

When we spent the night we always had prayer and Bible reading together as did they when we weren't there. Grandaddy used to say, "If you go to bed without *reading* (he meant reading from the Bible), you go to bed like the hogs". I recall much of what they said during that bedtime prayer. Its a prayer I incorporated each night with my son and still do: "...Father, let Connie and Cameron always walk the right road and look to you for guidance in whatever they may say and do...".

Proverbs 4:26,27 - "Ponder the path of thy feet, and let all thy ways be established. Turn not to the right hand nor to the left; remove thy foot from evil." (KJV)

Matthew 7:13,14 - "Enter through the narrow gate. For wide is the gate and broad is the road that leads to destruction, and many enter through it. But small is the gate and narrow the road that leads to life, and only a few find it." (NKJV)

A young child would have no idea what these words mean. the child would think of a literal path/gate. Possibly so might a new believer. I interpret this Scripture two ways: the broad road means hell and the narrow, heaven of course; but, for our walk on earth I believe it is referring to the choices we make while still in the flesh, moral choices. Following the world is easy, therefore the road would seem wide. Standing for righteousness is a lonely life sometimes and the road seems narrow and hard to pass at times. Many will disagree with me here Im sure but one thing comes to mind: drinking alcohol. Many Christians today find no fault in this as long as you don't get drunk. For me, I see drinking as something that associates itself more than anything almost with the "world". Why would I want anything that is like the "world". Why would I want to flirt with something that could be deadly to myself or others? An alcoholic started with one glass. It has the prospective possibility to be addictive and lead to even harder substances to get even higher. Why would I want to play with that? This is just my opinion and in no way am I casting aspersions.

As a young child I imagine the words in Grandmomma's prayer sounded like the teacher on "Peanuts" (Charlie Brown) to me, I imagine I had my mind going in a thousand different directions. Yet, it did sink into my spirit, for here I sit 35 plus years later able to recall it, able to see us there in the living room lit from the table lamp, with Grandmomma in her rocking chair, Grandaddy on the couch, and Connie and I on the floor. Oh to go back and be in that scene just once more! I wish I could remember more of the words of that prayer, but I'm thankful for that much.   See, I don't remember frowns from their faces from when we might have misbehaved, hearing "when will your parents ever get here", hearing deep breaths as we asked for something at the store... I don't remember any of that because it never took place! Frankly, I don't recall us misbehaving much if any, we respected them too much. To that I credit "them" more so than us. They were so giving, so kind, so gentle that it would've broken our hearts to hurt or disappoint them. What I do recall as far as facial expressions was, and I can see it so clearly in my mind now, Grandmomma's face and eyes every time we left, every time. Tears. Her eyes swelled with tears each time we left! She would smile her sweet, goodbye smile and there were those eyes, those precious eyes filled with tears. This from a woman who would see us the very next day, every day. [Oh, grandparents please, please see the blessings that you have and treasure them.

Grandmomma and Grandaddy were gentle, giving, humorous... the list could go on indefinitely. Our grandaddy was a big, tower of a man, yet as gentle as a lamb with us. He was strong when needed and extremely stubborn. A perfect picture if you will, of how a Godly man should love his wife and his family and care for them. This is what I would call agape love. Agape love is not friend or brotherly love, but its sacrificial love. It shows action. God's agape love is in believers only. As believers we should do all things with the love of God expecting nothing in return.

Agape Love defined:

1 John 4:8,9 - "Whoever does not love does not know God, because God is love. This is how God showed His love for us- He sent His only Son into the world that we might live through Him." (NIV)

John 3:16 - "For God so loved the world that He gave His only begotten son that whosoever believes in Him should not perish but have everlasting life." (KJV)

Romans 5:8 - "God showed His great love for us by sending Christ to die for us while we were still sinners." (NLT)

Grandaddy was also in covenant love with Grandmomma and all of us. As such, his job was to protect us and love us. This was his God-commanded job. I could run to Grandaddy to feel safe if I was afraid and yet he was gentle if I was sad or hurt. When I try to put Grandaddy into words I think of Psalm 91 and Proverbs 14:26 abbr.-

"He who dwells in the shelter of the Most High will abide in the shadow of the Almighty. I will say to the Lord, "My refuge and my fortress, my God, in whom I trust." For he will deliver you from the snare of the fowler and from the deadly pestilence. He will cover you with his pinions, and under his wings you will find refuge; his faithfulness is a shield and buckler. You will not fear the terror of the night, nor the arrow that flies by day, ... because he holds fast to me in love, I will deliver him, I will protect him, because he knows my name... ." (ESV)

"In the fear of the Lord is strong confidence: and his children shall have a place of refuge. " (KJV)

I believe God intends us to fashion ourselves after Him. Those verses were of course speaking of God. My grandaddy tried daily to fashion his life after Christ. It is a daily walk, a daily journey. Each day we need to wake up thanking and praising God and seeking Him and His

Will for us in all we say and do.   Grandaddy never woke thinking, "I'm old, I'm bored, I'm frail, I can't..." Regardless of our age, we need to ask God daily, "God, what do you need me to do today, what will you have me do, can I be a help to anyone today, this is the day you made us all and I will rejoice and be glad in it..." Look at the heroes of faith in the Old Testament: Moses was 80 before God used him to lead the Israelites out of Egypt.   Job was estimated to be 60 when he lost everything and yet started over and lived another 140 years.   Caleb was 40 when he went to spy out the land of Canaan. David was a teen (some say 16 give or take) when he killed Goliath. God used a boy to feed a multitude.   And lest we forget one of the miracles of the Bible- Sarah gave birth to her first child in her 90's and Abraham was near if not 100!   Point being, God uses us at any age, young or old.

Grandaddy was a giant full of faith up until his last breath.   I recall a terrible time in his life.   He contracted gangrene in his feet.   A condition, I imagine brought on by his diabetes.   It causes the tissue to die.   It was a horrible case of it.   His doctor said to save his legs and possibly worse, his feet would have to be amputated.   Grandaddy didn't flinch.   He grabbed that ferocious faith and said, "No!   If God wanted my feet cut off He'd take them off".   We laughed at that years later, not at the seriousness of his condition, but with joy at his great faith in the Lord.   He knew that the spirit of gangrene was not what controlled his destiny.   And yes, I believe diseases are a spirit.   [Luke 13:11- " *...there was a woman which had a spirit of infirmity...* " (KJV);

15

the NASB even says, *"...woman who for eighteen years had a sickness caused by a spirit..."*.] When I say, "spirit", I do NOT mean demon possessed so please don't go away thinking I am saying all the sick are demon possessed. That is not at all what I am saying or believe. God often refers to sickness in the Bible as a spirit. Nor do I believe sickness is a judgment of sin. Yes, often times our sin can open the door to disease, calamity, or disasters, of course. Sexual immorality/perversion can open the door to disease as proven scientifically not to mention Biblically. Gluttony, abuse of substances, stress, lack of sleep, worry, poor eating habits, the list goes on and on can also open that door. That's why the Bible makes it clear that our bodies are a temple of God and to be treated so both physically and spiritually to guard against the enemy's access mentally, physically, and spiritually. I think you get my point. Disease/illness is not given to us by God. God doesn't send disease upon us. God never intends us to be ill, depressed, lack,... Matthew 12:15 says, ...a large crowd followed Him and He healed some; but, the terminal diseases, the blind, the crippled, the deceased, He just took pity on.

Did you just frown or get upset? I hope that stirred you because PRAISE GOD that's NOT what the Scripture said! It says, "a large crowd followed Him and He healed ALL who were sick, lame, and afflicted." The same was recorded in Luke 6:19 and Matthew 15:30. There are 30+ verses that speak of Jesus healing them ALL. There isn't one account of Jesus denying healing or failing to be able even after death. The same power is given to all believers so all of which is

16

just as possible today. (Mark 3:15, Romans 6:10-11, Ephesians 1:19-20, John 14:12-14). The power that was in Jesus when He walked this earth is the same power He left us in His Name!

Jesus said in John 16:33 that we will have troubles/trials/difficulties/ testings but we are to "take heart I have overcome the world". Thankfully as a believer, we are in this world but not of this world. God has given us the armor to combat what this evil world throws at us. Jesus said "greater works will you do than I". Let's take the authority He bestowed. Let's speak health, prosperity, protection, and peace over our households daily. Let us not waste the gift that Christ died to give us. Let us be bold to share our faith (the Gospel, the plan of salvation), walk in love, encourage, and yes, lay hands on the sick and expect a miracle.

During testing/trials we should use that time to reflect and draw closer to Jesus, to ask Him to show us ways we can improve. And above all during storms never worry, complain, doubt or be angry at the Lord. Again, satan intends tragedies for harm, yet God can turn them into good. I often say to Burns, "When satan attacks, just laugh at him. Sooner or later he'll say to himself and his demons, 'hey, leave them alone, it's not worth the trouble'."

As for our diseases, Jesus paid that price on the cross. With each stripe He healed our diseases. [Isaiah 53:5- ..."*with his stripes we are healed*" (KJV); Matthew 8:17- "*That is might be fulfilled which was spoken by Isaiah saying, Himself took our infirmities, and bare*

17

our sicknesses." (KJV) The NASB says, "*carried away our diseases.*"

Jesus took 39 stripes- there are 39 major categories of diseases. Coincidence? There is no Hebrew word for coincidence. God is methodical and nothing is Scripture is there by chance. There are tons of mysteries hidden throughout Scripture.

I apologize for getting into that so much. Its a book on its own and hard to mention without a little explanation.

Now to describe Grandmomma. She was extremely gentle, intelligent, patient... She was the epitome of GRACE! I often said to the children when I taught Sunday School that I know there aren't any perfect "people", but I knew someone, only one who came extremely close, if not succeeded- Grandmomma. Every day of her life was used. I hope someday that can be said of me. Its a goal to

Grand momma & Connie

aim for, for sure. Not to waste a day, wow. Not to waste it with laziness, complaining, hatred, worry... . How many can say that? Her love for the Lord, her sweet, gentle spirit was visible. She didn't live this way to flaunt herself. She lived that way simply because she was filled with the love of her Savior. I can sit here and boast all day long about her and every word would be deserved. She would never have boasted.

She went home to her Father in August 1981. She had cancer. Apparently from the stage at discovery, she'd had for some time. Not one time did she complain. It all happened so fast. It seemed one day she was in the house as normal and the next deathly ill in the hospital. I was young and not aware of much, but I remember hearing the doctor say, "she should be in pain, she should be feeling this". Yet, she didn't. She never complained, not once. God spared her that. I'll not give much time to that because that's surely not what defined her nor what I prefer to recall about her. I'll not give cancer that audience.

Her beauty came from within and made her face almost glow, daily! That's a hard feat to master with all the trials we face as humans. There is an old saying, one I believe: the eyes are the window to the soul. Grandmomma exuded beauty, Godly beauty, and light from those eyes.

Matthew 6:22,23- "If your eye is pure, there will be sunshine in your soul. But if your eye is clouded with evil thoughts and

19

desires, you are in deep spiritual darkness. And oh, how deep that darkness can be!" (TLB)

Today, *People* magazine and the like will have issues yearly that showcase "the most beautiful people..." Oh, how lacking and ignorant they are in the knowledge of what true beauty is. To put Grandmomma into words and to connect with Scripture is easy-Proverbs 31. There's a section particularly that I'd like to highlight:

"Charm is deceptive, and beauty is fleeting; but a woman who fears the Lord is to be praised." (NIV)

Also, Psalm 29:2:

"Give unto the Lord the glory due to His name; Worship the Lord in the beauty of His holiness." (NKJV)

" 'Her' beauty is that of the hidden person of the heart; 'she' has the incorruptible beauty of a gentle and quiet spirit."~ Gene Taylor

Proverbs 13:22 - "A good man leaveth an inheritance to his children's children..." (KJV)

All of us as parents/grand have to decide what legacy we will leave. Is it a Kingdom legacy? To me, this verse has both physical (natural) and spiritual meanings. As far as the natural, making money and saving money for your children is great and is Scriptural too, but not in lieu of spiritual treasure. Teaching your children faith in the Lord, how to love Him, how to live for Him is your responsibility. I recently heard a preacher say that in the last days, faith will be more valuable to have than money. We can already begin to see a glimpse of this as normal is becoming increasingly abnormal and visa versa. What would have been seen as barbaric just a few short years ago is now vogue within the world. We used to say "20 years ago, 50.." we would never have believed such would happen/be accepted/be lawful... Now I catch myself seeing things changing at such a rapid pace I now say, "a month ago I wouldn't have believed I'd see...".

Proverbs 4:27 - "Turn not to the right hand or the left; remove thy foot from evil." (KJV)

Revelation 3:16 - "So because you are lukewarm, and neither hot or cold, I will spit you out of my mouth." (ESV)

In plain language, quit playing both sides of the fence. Quit dabbling in worldly things and claiming Jesus from the same tongue. Example: Your purse (you) that you take to church on Sunday may be beautiful but look at the trash that's hiding inside that you drag out when you get home: filthy language, inappropriate entertainment, resentment, un-forgiveness, anger, sexual immorality, quarreling, gossiping ETC, and ETC. Remember your children watch you, they will be you one day. Ok with that? Ok with how God sees you now? I'm preaching to the mirror too. I wake each day and see it as a new start. Growing never ends, learning new revelation from the Word never ends, maturing in the Faith never ends. Never let satan get you by recalling the past. Condemnation is not from God. Forgiveness and remembering confessed sin no more are from God.

I recently found this wonderful prayer for parents. I've always prayed over, with, and for Burns but I wish I had this when he was born. I adapted it a little to fit us:

Father, in the name of Jesus, I pray and confess Your Word over Burns and surround Burns with my faith- faith in Your Word that You watch over it to perform it! I confess and believe that my Burns is a disciple of Christ taught of the Lord and obedient to Your will. Great is the peace and undisturbed composure of Burns, because of You, God, contend with that which contends with Burns, and give Burns safety and ease him. Allow Burns to lack no good thing an earthly father can give. Allow him to seek You as his heavenly and earthly father, guider, protector, and provider of wisdom and favor. Cause Burns to seek to know you, to have an unction to be close to you that only the Holy Spirit can provide. Cause him to be a pure giant, a soldier for your laws, someone who never wavers. He will never be lukewarm.

Father, You will perfect that which concerns me. I commit and cast the care of Burns once and for all over on you, Father. Burns is in Your hands, and I am positively persuaded that You are able to guard and keep that which I have committed to You. You are more than enough!

I confess that Burns obeys me in the Lord as His representative, because this is just and right. Burns will honor, esteem, and value as precious me as his parent; for this is the first commandment with a promise: that all may be well with him and that he may live a long, abundant, and healthy life. I believe and confess that Burns choose love and love You, Lord, obey Your voice, and cling to You; for You are his life and the length of his days. Therefore, Burns is the head and not the tail, and shall be

23

above only and not beneath. He is blessed when he comes in and when he goes out.

I believe and confess that You give Your angels charge over Burns to accompany and defend and preserve him in all his ways. You, Lord, are his refuge and fortress. You are his glory and the lifter of his head.

As his parent, I will not provoke, irritate, or fret him. I will not be hard on him or harass him, or cause him to become discouraged, sullen, morose, or feel frustrated. I will not break or wound his spirits, but will rear him tenderly in the training, discipline, counsel, and admonition of the Lord. I will train him in the way he should go, and when his is old he will not depart from it.

O Lord, my Lord, how excellent is Your name in all the earth! You have set Your glory on or above the heavens. Out of the mouth of babes and unweaned infants You have established strength because of Your foes, that You might silence the enemy and the avenger. I sing praise to Your name, O Most High. The enemy is turned back from Burns in the name of Jesus! Burns increases in wisdom and in favor with God and man. Amen!
- adapted from BillWinstonMinistries.com

Proverbs 22:6 - "Train up a child in the way he should go and when he is old, he will not depart from it." (KJV)

Never underestimate your power/influence on your grandchildren. If you feel you failed as a parent, what a great opportunity God gives grandparents. This is your 2nd chance. Parents often get so busy with financial issues, work, schedules.... Step in. Step up. Get involved. Most of all, pray for these "gifts" God has given. I heard of a man who said, "the best part of your grandchildren's visit is seeing the tail lights". I don't know his heart, perhaps he just had no clue what that sounded like. I hope so. But, as we've learned, watch your words, even your jesting. There are plenty of parents/grandparents out there who have prematurely lost a child or aren't able to see theirs and would give anything to see

Grandaddy, Cameron, Grandmomma, & Connie

those lights once more. In this dark world, these little children need so much love, so much care, so much tenderness, so much understanding, so much grace. It matters not how rambunctious yours are, how much they eat when they come, how much

25

they break... They are precious vessels that need you, need your
wisdom, need your gentle hands/arms wrapped around them and
often.

Chapter 3
Precious Memories, Stored up Treasure

*C*onnie and I grew up in a "Shangri-La" if you will. An excess of

money we didn't have, but I always thought and still today think we had it all, we were rich! I can't think of a single bad memory during that time of our lives, not one! We lost Grandmomma and Grandaddy early, or it was early for Connie and I for sure. I was just barely 10 and Connie 14. Grandmomma went home in August of 1981 and Grandaddy just 6 months later. A huge chunk of our hearts left during that terrible time. Yet, we carried the greatest of gifts with us our whole life: precious memories, a Godly legacy, no regrets, and a feeling as I mentioned earlier of being the richest children in the world. Their legacy continues to their great grandson, my son Burns Homer. He hears and has heard of them often. I keep their memory alive. I keep their morals alive, I keep their spirits alive in him. He often asks, "Momma, is this like Grandaddy Homer, is that?"

If it is he just lights up knowing he is like him in any way. Grandaddy was a good cook but super messy. Burns takes after him in that way as well, makes me laugh and smile all the while cleaning up after the tornado.

Food for thought: the way we talk to our children becomes their inner voice.

A quote from an unknown, wise mother- "Let me love you a little more before you're not little anymore."

I can't start Connie's story even yet without mentioning our parents. The description of them is not unlike Grandmomma and Grandaddy's. Different people yes, different personalities yes, but much the same core qualities. We again were blessed, blessed with Godly parents so the "richness" continued. As I grew older I began to see we were reared a bit strict/different in that we couldn't do some of the things our friends did. While in that moment, I never recall resenting it. As a matter of fact, I liked it. I felt safe, loved, and super cared for. I remember using the spinner from my LIFE game while at my cousin's house because I wasn't allowed to play with dice even in a board game. We couldn't play with cards and were very limited on what we could watch on TV. The shows were so tame then compared to now. We heard no foul language and were never exposed to alcohol of any kind. Those are just a few things that we were exposed to and shielded from that may seem strange to some. Now that I am an adult I appreciate that so much and have chosen to rear my son with the same values and expectations. As a result, I already see in him great, strong, Godly traits that I pray will follow him all the days of his life and continue to strengthen.

My parents and grandparents were not of the school to "go with the crowd" or care about what the popular thing was to do at the time. Instead, they felt pleasing God was the most important thing and that is not always the popular or the up-to-date way in the eyes of the world. Frankly, in many cases its considered strange and mocked, even among Christians. I was thinking of this recently when Momma and I were talking about realizing times change but morals do not. God does not change nor do His expectations. He wrote one Bible and had no plans of adjusting it to fit "the times" in the way of dumbing down, watering down morality. Future lifestyles and customs did not take God by surprise nor catch Him unawares. I said that I expected the same from Burns as...(I thought a while and said) "Isaac" (I was just trying to make the point that time doesn't matter with morality). My son, Burns overheard that and although wise beyond his years didn't quite get that. I explained that yes, the world has advanced and we do things in a modern way that generations before didn't even dream of;

God calls us to be "light" in the world...

Picture a field of hay or wheat with one single row of beautiful, bold, purple lavender. Which are you going to notice/admire, which changes the landscape? Dare I add, which gets mowed down and even dies when the season has passed?

Lavender's stems remain upright through the winter in preparation for new spring growth...hmmm but, God expects the same from him as He did me, my parents, and every generation back to Adam.

Romans 12:2 - "Do not be conformed to this world, but be ye transformed by the renewal of your mind, that by testing you may discern what is the will of God, what is good and acceptable and perfect." (ESV)

Let me say now that Connie and I didn't always make the best or right choices. We aren't perfect. Parents can do their absolute best and children can still stray and make mistakes. But at least in our case, we always felt that nudge to do the right thing. That nudge came from our upbringing before salvation and the Holy Spirit after. But boy, the spiritual seeds that were planted in us ran deep and were always right there to guide us and mold us into the adults we became.

Psalms 1:3 - "And he shall be like a tree planted by rivers of water, that bringeth forth fruit in his season, his leaf shall not wither, and whatsoever he doeth shall prosper." (KJV)

Notice "whatsoever" (whatever)- that includes everything.

"The grace of God even makes my mistakes to prosper" ~ Charles Capps

Momma over the years often mentioned a tiny little thing about Connie as a little girl. She had a strong desire to go to church when she was very little. Momma often recalls a time when Connie was sick and wasn't able to go how she cried and begged Momma to let her go anyway. As

Momma and Connie

I think about that it just proves so many things. Proves that bringing up a child in a loving and prayerful environment molds that child. Parents may see this planted seed develop early on and sometimes not until much later in life. Connie's life just like anyone took many turns, many mistakes were made, many regrets, but she ALWAYS had that "planted seed" in her that nudged her, convicted her, and in the end restored her.

I can not stress enough the power of a faithful example in parents/ grandparents and what an impact it makes on a child to be covered in prayer. I know because I am that child. I am so tempted to take this in another direction and write about these morals and get deeper into that spiritual teaching, but I will have to save that for another time. I want this to be about Connie and the miracles we've been blessed with. I realize I have already taken more time than I probably should have. I have to say that without the hedge of prayer and walk with the Lord that came before us, I wonder if we would even be privy to these miraculous things I'm about to reveal.

Chapter 4
Just Connie

Jeremiah 29:11 - "For I know the plans I have for you, declares the Lord, plans for good and not evil, to give you a future and a hope." (TLB)

*I*ts hard to begin the actual story of *Connie's Miracles*. It has

taken me months to be emotionally ready to write. Even now, I'm not sure I can do them justice or convey them in written form. Its hard to know where to even start. I almost think I should begin by telling a bit of Connie's story prior to these miracles, a bit of her background as a young adult. I think that will make part of the story more clear.

Connie was always a hard worker. She worked during high school and during her last 3 years of college: worked full time, was married, and went to school full time. As for her future interests in a possible career, that was to be based on her heart for the elderly, birthed solely on Grandmomma and Grandaddy's memory.

During college the Lord led her to work at the local hospital. She started in the ER at night, dispatching, then would drive 45 minutes to college the next day (one way). She impressed many while at the hospital and it didn't take long to be promoted to various positions. She ended up working in her dream department, the elderly psychiatric unit; although, she didn't begin with that. She majored in Psychology because she knew one day, not sure how, that she would help the elderly in some way connected to this. I want to mention now even though it may be a bit premature, Connie was not saved at this time. She, like many "thought" she had accepted the Lord as Savior when young. So thankful that even though she was lost, the Lord was still in charge of directing her paths.

Proverbs 3:4 - "So shalt thou find favor and good understanding in the sight of God and man." (KJV)

Its amazing to me how God plans our paths even when we haven't accepted Him as Savior yet or have wandered away. I've seen and heard this same story in so many testimonies. How if God hadn't led them "here" or allowed "this" to happen... What a loving and patient God we have the privilege to serve. God never gives up on us even though we give up as do the ones around us. One of the greatest ways to describe God is that of a parent.

Matthew 7:11 - "If you then, who are evil, know how to give good gifts to your children, how much more will your Heavenly Father give good gifts to those who ask Him." (ESV)

*We are all His children and just as our earthly parents are to love us unconditionally, oh how much more does God?! I'm so thankful He was patient with Connie, me...*ALL OF US

Many reading this may already know about "salvation". Even people who have been reared in a Christian home may have missed the true meaning. Connie for one had been reared in a Christian environment, attended a Christian school, yet the true meaning of giving your heart and life to Jesus escaped her for so long. John 3 is an excellent chapter to read to understand salvation. I will put it in simple terms: You are a sinner, you were born that way, we all were. Accept that and accept that Jesus is God's son, He died on the cross for you and rose again. He is alive today. Believe that He is Lord, ask Him in prayer to come into your heart, forgive you, and be the Lord of your life. Ask Him to wash your heart and make it pure. From that moment on you are a child of God and you will have a desire to learn more about Him, to live for Him. Find a church that preaches the truth, find another Christian who can mentor you. Read the Bible daily for yourself, pray often and while doing so, ask God to help you learn, help you grow to be the man/woman He wants you to be. Remember this: the second you accept Jesus and repent, He washes ALL your sins away and remembers them no more! Satan loves to get to you however he can and one way he loves to is through self condemnation.

Psalm 103:12 - "He has removed our sins as far away from us as the east is from the west." (TLB)

There is no sinner too "bad" to save. God accepts you just the way you are BUT thank God, DOES NOT LEAVE US THAT WAY.

John 8:11 - "*...go, and sin no more.*" (KJV)

There are only 2 after death destinations regardless of what Hollywood or the ignorant elite (excuse the candor) like to fool you into believing- heaven and hell. With Jesus in your heart you are promised heaven, without, you are assured of hell. Also contrary to the "elite", Jesus Christ is the ONLY way to heaven. Acts 16:31 says, "*...believe on the Lord Jesus and you will be saved.*" Simple.

Being a good person is great and should be a goal, but it will not save you. There will be many in hell who have gone to church, given, been a good person, taught the Bible... yet unless they've asked Jesus in their hearts He will say to them, "*Depart from me, I do not know you.*" - Matthew 7:21-23. Don't put it off, call on Jesus. Jesus makes it so simple, so easy: "*Everyone who calls on my name will be saved.*" -Romans 10:13. Remember: None of us are promised another breath.

I realize I got off Connie's story a bit and I may again, but I need to add things as God lays them on my heart albeit perhaps a strange location in the story.

Now back to our story.

Connie had caught the attention of the head counselor while at the hospital. She, unbeknownst to Connie went to the director of the hospital recommending he not only hire Connie to be a counselor, but to pay her tuition and to keep that position open until Connie graduated! After graduation, Connie walked right into that position and loved every minute, although challenging. It was a drug and alcohol unit. Her passion was the elderly though and the Lord wasn't about to ignore that. That unit eventually faded out and another company moved in. Guess what kind-

A geriatric psychiatric unit! Now Connie had her dream! She began as a counselor and not long after was promoted to the director. Keep in mind, she only had a bachelor's degree. This position called for a masters at the least. Again, nothing is impossible with hard work and most of all, the Lord! She thrived at this position. She enjoyed it so and was loved by her staff and the patients. She was allowed to name the unit. She chose "Senior Care" (please remember this name for later). She treasured this job, "Senior Care"! Senior Care defined her, completed her, at least that part of her. After a few years she was "called on the carpet", not for what you might expect- she hadn't taken a vacation, sick day, or any time off for over two years. She enjoyed it so, she hated to not be there. The heads of the company laughed at the unusualness of this "problem" but said she had to take a vacation or they'd get in trouble. I recall that time, she was miserable being at home- missing those patients. I say all that not to brag on her, but to help lay the foundation for what occurs later.

Psalm 68:19 - " Blessed be the Lord, who daily loads us with benefits..." (KJV)

I love that word "loads"! I don't know about you but I'm so thankful that God's hands never run out of room, never tire of holding us, never tire of helping us. I'm so thankful that He "loads" us down if we'll just trust Him.

I've been on a personal journey for a few years now. A journey (revelation) I'm ashamed to say came to me this late in life. I've been learning about God's plan for us. When He died on the cross He not only paid the price for our salvation but He also paid for our healing, joy, prosperity... He wants us whole in every arena. As I reflect back on this favor Connie had professionally, I am reminded of many verses that speak of His favor to us:

Psalms 115:12-16 - "The Lord remembers us and will bless us..." (NIV)

Psalm 84:11 - "...the Lord bestows favor and honor. No good thing does he withhold from those who walk uprightly." (NIV)

Isaiah 53:5 - "...with his stripes we are healed." (KJV)

Jeremiah 29:11 - "For I know the plans I have for you declares the Lord, plans to prosper you..." (NIV)

Philippians 4:19 - "And my God shall supply all my needs according to His riches in glory through Christ Jesus." (KJV)

Psalm 34:10 - "...those who seek the Lord lack no good thing." (KJV)

11 Corinthians 9:8 - "God is able to make all grace abound toward you; that ye, always having all sufficiency in all things, may abound to every good work." (KJV)

1 Corinthians 1:27 - "But God has selected (for His purpose) the foolish things of the world to shame the wise (revealing their ignorance), and God has selected (for His purpose) the weak things of the world to shame the things which are strong (revealing their frailty)." (AMP)

These verses have really been my anthem during this journey. Many times I feel foolish and feel like the stand I take and the things I do or don't do must seem foolish to some. I particularly imagine some of the decisions I have made must seem foolish to others. To know that God uses this very thing for His glory makes me feel empowered and safe to say the least. Its awesome knowing you're on God's side! Many times in Scripture, God asked people to do foolish seeming acts of obedience. Many times He chose who or even what (a donkey once) was foolish to others to do His work.

He elevates us professionally and socially many times to advance the Kingdom:

John 17:26 - "...and I have made your name known to them, and will continue to make it known, so that the love with which you have loved me may be in them (overwhelming their heart) and I (may be) in them." (AMP)

Chapter 5
Change

During this time, Connie was married. She married during
college. She had married this man for life. They had dated for 6
years and were married for 4 years. She loved him unconditionally.
They lived almost all their married life in the guest house behind our
house. Just months before their 4th anniversary, they finally moved
into a house of their own. They had it built; Connie was so excited.
She had her home, the man she loved, and a fulfilling career.
Sadly, that part of her life began to take an ugly turn. She hadn't even
finished decorating or unpacking completely when she discovered he
had been unfaithful to her. She had suspicions before, but he had
always convinced her and the rest of us that we had it wrong. We
discovered after the divorce that he had never been faithful even
during the dating years. She was hit terribly hard with this loss. It
was as a death to her which escalated over time. She had married him
for life and had never dreamed of not keeping **her** vows. You all
know the phrase: the truth shall set you free- in this case I think

about the two of them and anyone in a adulterous marriage. I've seen several cases, some where the woman was the victim and some the man. I've also had the chance to observe the outcomes over the years and follow them. With most of the cases, the adulterer seemed to have it all at first, but in time, the tables turned. That was the case here as well. God will judge.

Luke 8:17 - "For nothing is secret, that shall not be made manifest; neither anything hid, that shall not be known and come out." (KJV)

Hebrews 13:4 - "Marriage is honorable in all, and the bed undefiled; but, whoremongers and adulterers God will judge." (KJV)

Its hard for us watching not to judge. I spent many years hating my former brother in law. Actually, I was just recently released from that. Who was I hurting- just me (and the Holy Spirit). Who was I helping- no one. I saw what this man did to my sister and that's how I justified my hate. I should've hated the sin but not the sinner. For who was I once, but a sinner as well and

Matthew 7:1 - "Judge not, that ye be not judged." (KJV)

now saved by grace, a new creature. I should've prayed for him.

Matthew 5:44 - "But I tell you to love your enemies and pray for anyone who mistreats you." (CEV)

43

There are tons of scriptures that speak of forgiving. The main one I think of is:

Matthew 6:14,15 - "For if you forgive other people when they sin against you, your heavenly Father will also forgive you. But if you do not forgive others their sins, your Father will not forgive your sins." (NIV)

That verse there stands alone. The enemy will use un-forgiveness against us so often. He'll innocently refer to it often as "hurt feelings". He'll even make you feel you have the right to hang on to this hurt. Hurt in these cases equates un-forgiveness no matter how its sugar-coated. When I mentioned the purse (you) you carry to church- this un-forgiveness can be in the form of a knife you carry with you. The knife represents the backstabber you can't forgive, the betrayal of the friend, relative, spouse... and the list goes on and on. It could represent the grudge you hold on another, the hurt you yourself caused and are continuing to cause.

Ephesians 4:31 - "Get rid of all bitterness, rage and anger, brawling and slander, along with every form of malice." (NIV)

"To be a Christian means to forgive the inexcusable because God has forgiven the inexcusable in you"- C.S. Lewis

Many years after their divorce, Connie got to that place too where she could forgive and pray for him. I think that was the first step in her healing from that. Marriage is a step far more important than we can realize until we are in it. So many enter unprepared. So many marry who "they" want and never consider who God has in mind-

Genesis 2:18- "*It is not good that man should be alone; I will make a helper fit for him.*" (KJV)

Before anyone gets ready to argue and say wait that was for Adam. Forgive me if my opinion is wrong, but I believe the Bible is for me from Genesis 1 to Revelation 22. I believe God meant every word for every person, every generation. So I believe if we'll seek Him out He will show us who our "fit" is. I've been guilty as well of not seeking Him, so I'm talking to the mirror here as well. I feel Connie would be the first to admit that she dated and married him for all the wrong reasons. Reasons that seemed worthy to her at the time, but in the end/bottom line- was not God's Plan.

Her heart was broken and began to break her spirit. We were aware but kept thinking time would "heal all wounds". Looking back now, we weren't as aware as we thought. We couldn't relate to this hurt nor were we inside her heart and head. We tried to see and understand and even help her heal, but we just weren't enough. I feel our main wrongdoing was we focused on making sure she just forgot and moved past. As I said, this was as a death to her. When you lose a loved one, are you just to pack them away and "go on" as if they never existed? I think that's what we thought she should/could do.

Not long after the divorce, she began to be not as much "Connie" in tiny steps. Too tiny, too gradual to alarm us.

She had *head knowledge* of Jesus and *read* the Bible (works alone), but as she discovered later, she didn't have the <u>relationship</u> coupled with that knowledge with her Heavenly Father that was vital during this time. Without that piece of the puzzle (without that <u>relationship</u>), you're left with just "religion" which is a "thing" and can not fill that void, heal that hurt or save.

If only we had known she was lost as well. We all assumed she was saved as did she even. That last statement may be a bit confusing. What in the world do I mean, "she even thought she was saved"? Having grown up in a Christ filled home/environment, you take church and sometimes even Christ Himself for granted. I liken it to a wealthy child who has never known anything, but plenty. A new bike, a new game doesn't mean much to them, the excitement isn't there as much. They don't long for money because there's an ample amount around them. They consider themselves rich even though they did nothing to earn that money, its just there, all around them. When they are grown they still think they're wealthy and it may not be until the parents stop dishing out the money that they realize, "hey, I don't have a dime, I'm going to have to earn this myself." Are they stupid for thinking this? I don't think so. Does this happen to all rich children/all from a faith-filled home? No, but it does to many. That's the best analogy I could think of to describe what Connie may have experienced and you too perhaps. I thought it myself for a time. Its very hard to put into words. I myself even though deep down I must have known better, known the truth, put off salvation. Is this also a tool satan uses? Yes. He knows what goes on in people's lives. He sneaks in wherever he can. The enemy owns nothings, no one belongs to him. He is a mere thief and has to steal what he gets and steal his followers. With Godly families he has to be a bit sneakier. What better way than to convince the product/ child of that home

1 Peter 5:8 - "Be sober, be vigilant; because your adversary the devil, as a roaring lion, walketh about, seeking whom he may destroy." (KJV)

that their parents are so good, salvation isn't even needed; that God in no way would turn them away, being reared so well.

What a dangerous enemy we have lurking. He can take on so many forms. He's not just this comic book dragon with a tail. He can appear just as gentle and sweet as a lamb.   He's out there "seeking whom he may devour."

Luke 10:19 - "Behold, I give unto you power to tread on serpents and scorpions, and over all the power of the enemy: {wow! thats my favorite part- we can stomp on that devil and command him to flee in the name of Jesus!} and nothing shall by any means hurt you." (KJV)

Thankfully, in 1996 at the age of 29, Connie was convicted by the Lord to examine her heart and she realized she was lost. She asked the Lord into her heart for the first time. She started to gain that inner happiness again that she had lost; honestly, that she had truly never had.

Revelation 3:20 - "Behold I stand at the door and knock, if anyone hears my voice and opens the door, I will come in..." (KJV)

Romans 10:13 - "For whosoever shall call upon the name of the Lord shall be saved." (KJV)

"God can't give us peace and happiness apart from Himself because there is no such thing." ~ C.S. Lewis

Connie began growing spiritually; but her health had already began taking a downward turn, unknown to any of us. Before this, she enjoyed great health, was very seldom sick with anything. She was strong, dependable...she was who we all turned to and leaned on. That part of our life, her life, was about to come to a screeching halt. The change became evident to all during the time our Daddy became ill. In 1998, Daddy went in for a routine checkup and found out he had to have quadruple bypass surgery. We had just taken Daddy to Memphis (his surgery was scheduled for the next day). Me, Momma, and Connie had gone back home for the night. We dropped Connie off at her apartment and had just gotten back home when we got a call that Connie was having a seizure! We raced to her apartment just as the ambulance was loading her. I'll never forget her face. She didn't know me or Momma. So, Momma had a husband in Memphis facing major surgery in the morning and a daughter in the local hospital with what we didn't know. They discovered she had suffered a full blown, tongue swallowing, life threatening seizure, her first. We did not know how long she would be in ICU, yet we had to get to Memphis and we had to keep Daddy in the dark. How to keep it from him, how to explain why Connie wasn't there?! The Lord took care of that for us. She was released soon and so was able to be at the hospital by the time Daddy was conscious.

She eventually "recovered" and never had that kind of seizure again but the seizures she did encounter, mediations for and the affects of continued and played havoc on her mind and body. Gone thankfully, were the major hospitalizing seizures, but she continued to have "minor" ones. Not so minor when they are happening though, a bit scary to her and anyone with her. She was able to work successfully for almost a year, but then the disease and more so the medicines to treat it began to take its toll. She began to lose track of time, black out, not be able to focus, and sit and stare as if napping with her eyes open. Once she stopped at a drive-in to get a soft drink right around lunch time. Thankfully, Daddy stopped in as well (hours later) and found her and knew something was wrong. She felt/thought she'd just pulled in/just arrived. She had no account for the time lost. She would sleep right through her alarm and habitually be late for work. Her work suffered as well, she just couldn't focus, couldn't take care of her tasks etc. All of which she couldn't help and was due to the seizure disorder and medications. Senior Care executives were extremely patient for as long as they could be.

James 1:2-4- "Consider it nothing but joy, my brothers and sisters, whenever you fall into various trials. Be assured that the testing of your faith (through experience) produces endurance (leading to spiritual maturity, and inner peace). And let endurance have its perfect result and do a thorough work, so that you may be perfect and completely developed (in your faith), lacking in nothing."

(AMP)

Romans 8:28- "And we know that for those who love God all things work together for good for those who are called according to His purpose." (ESV)

Her next heartbreak was about to hit. Due to her health, they had to ask her to resign. Her heart was shattered. Shattered too I think afraid her health might not ever be restored and where would that leave her career wise. And still, she was not over the heartbreak of losing her husband. She was determined to fight her illness. She just knew if she moved, got a fresh start, all would work itself out physically and mentally. She tried so hard! Breaks my heart even now remembering that time for her! Tons of things were against her, but she kept the faith and continued to fight. She moved out of state at first. Due to her awesome reputation and abilities she found employment rather quickly, but that ugly seizure disorder reared its ugly head too much and again another move. After all was said and done, she'd moved three more times. Eventually, we all could see, including her that she had to stop fighting it. Defeated career wise, she moved home with Momma and Daddy and later was awarded disability. What a blow to a girl who dreamed of a "career", had it, lost it, and knew she'd probably never have again. Living with my parents must have been so hard on her. A grown woman with so many health issues and still a broken heart and probably what seemed to her a loveless, jobless future.

During this time with my parents, sickness hit hard again. She was diagnosed with a grapefruit size tumor in her femur. It was so embedded in the bone, the doctor thought amputation was the only way to safely remove it. We began praying of course and she found a doctor at UAMS that was the only one doing her kind of surgery. He was able to remove the tumor and save her leg. But, just like the seizures, she was never free of the affects of that. She had horrific, debilitating pain and often. She had more metal, rods, concrete, and pins in that area than natural pieces. At one point, the doctors said her next step was a pain pump. Years of emotional pain and physical pain ate up her life. This was basically unknown to anyone other than us and her dearest and best friend, Renee. No one would have ever

51

believed the torment Connie was suffering. I don't use the term "torment" for just a dramatic affect. She was tormented! She suffered great bouts of depression as well. It would overtake her at times. She was human and even though she had the Lord, she fell at times and got weak. I imagined and feared thoughts of ending her life must have come to mind as bad as she was. My fears were correct, she battled with those feelings and often. At times it was like living with a kettle ready to boil, you just never knew what that next phone call might bring.

Isaiah 41:13 - "For I the Lord thy God will hold thy right hand, saying unto thee, Fear not: I will help thee." (KJV)
This is what we held onto, this was enough, this was all we had, this was enough!

This was known to me and my parents, yet we kept it hidden and never voiced it aloud even to each other. I guess we thought if it was voiced it would be real and reality wasn't something we could face with all of this. This torment trickled onto our parents, of course most of all too living with this, seeing her in such pain physically and mentally. They had to watch their daughter suffer physically and emotionally. It would be so bad so often that it was hard to recognize "Connie". I don't mean it altered her appearance, it altered "her". In some ways it paralyzed her emotionally which led to many times being confined to the bed and physically not being able to get up among many other things. Her mood swings were so very drastic and hard to understand and cope with at times. The medicine would make her at times live in another reality. She'd imagine things and situations that to her seemed so real. There is so much more to say about that, but I am not going to give any more attention to that awful time of her life. That was not my "Connie" and I'll not give that spirit of infirmity a platform by writing one more word of it.

 I remember my parents through these years, it almost crippled their spirits as well and yet no one on the "outside" knew. In a way, it was as if they lived in a glass house, constantly afraid it would break. Some would argue and say people should voice their troubles and let fellow Christians help by praying. I don't disagree, but in this case, they chose to go through it alone.   I recall Momma saying she herself had trouble getting out of bed at times, afraid to face the day. It had to be forced at times, hard to go places, hard to be involved with people. Momma even began avoiding a friend because she just couldn't face ever being asked "how is Connie?". If not for their faith and the strength and grace the Lord gave them, I'm not sure how they could've lived. This went on for eight long years. To see them at church, at the store you'd have no clue what they were dealing

1 Peter 5:6,7 - " Humble yourselves, therefore, under the mighty hand of God so that at the proper time He may exalt you, casting all your anxieties on Him, because He cares for you!" (ESV)

with. We all suffered, worried, cried, feared... but still to this day with all that we felt and went through it was nothing compared to what Connie endured. There's no way to describe what she went through without taking each day of her life and revealing it as a diary/ journal. As close as we were to the trouble, I know we had no inkling of the hell on earth Connie faced each day. As I see it now, its like she woke each day and had to fight– had to fight debilitating depression, debilitating pain, worrying about her future financially and emotionally. She felt little by little she was losing ground as a person; no one seemed to need her, no one seemed to trust her, no one seemed to look up to her anymore. She used to be the one we all turned to for so many things. She was now the invalid that caused nothing but heartache now and worry. Did we tell her that? Of course not, but put yourself in her shoes, that is how it would seem to anyone regardless of what we said or did. It was a bad situation no matter how you look at it. {Oh to have known then what I do now about the healing power of God. My eyes were blind to so many things then. I lacked so much knowledge. I could blame my parents, the school, the church... None of those are to blame. I take full responsibility. I had the Word, I had access to the Holy Spirit. I was content to browse the Word. I was content to read it verses letting it minister to me. I was content to stop where my outside teaching stopped. I was content to be fed by those sources instead of letting the Word feed me and enlighten me.}

For Connie, something had to give, something had to change! This girl needed a miracle!

Chapter 6
Just Praise

Isaiah 40:31 - "They that wait upon the Lord shall renew their strength; they shall mount up with wings as eagles; they shall run, and not be weary; and they shall walk, and not faint." (KJV)

A miracle was needed, a miracle was prayed for, a miracle was

expected!

Psalm 37:4 - "Delight thyself also in the Lord: and He shall give thee the desires of thine heart." (KJV)

Jeremiah 29:11 - "For I know the plans I have for you, says the Lord. They are plans for good and not evil, to give you a hope and a future." (TLB)

As I mentioned earlier (saying, "I wish I had known then what I do today about healing"), something I should've known for decades is that God does not intend any of us to be ill, be sad, or be in lack financially. We all from our early childhood know and are taught that it is not His Will "that any should perish but all have eternal life". He paid for our complete "wholeness" on the cross: our eternal salvation in addition to our emotional, physical, and financial wellbeing. We have to exercise the "measure of faith" (Romans 12:3) that we were all given when we accepted Jesus as Savior. In my ignorance I used to say: we're not promised anything past salvation. Hosea 4:6 says "my people are **destroyed** from lack of knowledge...", how true!

Looking back I see how knowing this would've helped us all, Connie especially. I wonder how many others if their eyes were willing to be opened... I can say this boldly because I myself was guilty. of this lack of knowledge!

In 2011 Connie began a major transformation! Our old "Connie" was coming back! The Lord was doing a work and a miracle was headed her way! A miracle in healing and a miracle in happiness. A Connie we hadn't seen since the early 90's! She wasn't 100% yet, but boy what a change! During most of the years she had lived with our parents (prior to her healing) she wasn't able to do "normal" every day activities. She never went to church. She would make arrangements with friends occasionally, but invariably be unable to go. She would make plans to come here and not be able or after getting here be unable to return home. It was horrible as I mentioned earlier! During those years, I felt my sister had literally died. I actually grieved her!!! It took me a long time to get over that even when she began healing.   I can say now, it took me TOO LONG!   Me and my parents had to just lay her on the alter <u>daily.</u> There was always though even during these dark years, a light (one of human form). That light had a name: Burns Homer Clark, my little boy.

No matter how she felt, she   was always able (miraculously) to be "Aunt Connie" to him. She never

failed him. She would be in immense pain and yet hold him, laugh with him, play with him, swim with him, talk with him etc. I can remember many times while here she would have to lay down and I can still hear her tell him to wake her when he was ready to play etc. I could always see the pain in her face yet with him

 she'd have that smile. I remember tears even; yet there was that smile. Even now, he would have no idea she was ever that sick during his lifetime. He knew she tired easily and had to take naps a lot, but he never saw what we did. How she was able to pull that off is impossible really, but as believers we know God made it possible. I'm more than thankful to the Lord that Burns will only have awesome memories. Burns will carry those memories forever I hope and I will do my best to make sure he's reminded.

During this healing time, she went back to the same doctor that said her next step was a pain pump. Guess what, he was floored that now she only needed over the counter pain or minor pain reliever as needed! He was amazed to say the least and Connie let him know quickly who was to receive the Glory! She began getting stronger and stronger emotionally and physically. She began being able to attend church and enjoying it. Don't let me mislead, she wasn't healed entirely, she still had her moments, but boy what a transformation and miracle. Before, she had more bad days than good and praise God now it was the opposite. She had truly lived in a storm for over 15 years. I'm tempted to say we all joined her, but I can't. Even though hard for us, its only torture, true torture for the one living it. I'm reminded of a time in the Bible God stopped the storm. I've heard the story and read it many times, yet not until recently did I see something I'd missed all this time. When Jesus and the disciples were in the boat, Jesus was asleep. It wasn't until recently that I saw or noticed where Jesus was in the boat. He was asleep at the stern- the driver's seat for lack of a better term! Once that sunk into me it really spoke to me. To me, that shows that in the midst of our storm it may seem God isn't listening, that He doesn't even care. Yet, He's so at peace that He can rest. He can rest in peace because He's already on the other side and He sees the shore, the peaceful shore, He's even standing on it. If we trust Him, He'll take the "wheel", after all, that's where He is and was all along! All we have to do while the storm rages is look at Him, walk toward Him, have faith in Him that He will steer us to safety. That's so simple, yet here I sit having known that story all my life and missed that truth. For some of us, our storms may last a bit longer than He intends, be rougher than He intends, or worse yet never end simply because we didn't use our faith, we stumbled, we had unconfessed sin, we took our eyes off of Him, we thought we could do it alone, we worried, we thought we could do it with the world's answers/the world's way...

Mark 4:35-41 abbr. - "And He arose, and rebuked the wind, and said unto the sea. Peace, be still. And the wind ceased, and there was great calm. And He said unto them, Why are you so fearful? How is it that ye have not faith?" (KJV)

I"ll interject a truth I discovered just recently regarding "storms" both physical and emotional: the world has always termed natural disasters as "acts of God". Insurance companies site the cause of damage "acts of God". The above verse says that Jesus rebuked the storm. Jesus wouldn't/couldn't rebuke anything given or created by the Father. Natural disasters show how our natural world is nearing the end; the results of Adam's fall is becoming more and more evident as this world is wearing out. It's another way the enemy perverts what he can to destroy. (Revelation 12:12, Romans 8:19-22) The same goes for personal "storms".

Ephesians 6:12 - "For we wrestle not against flesh and blood, but against principalities, against powers of this dark world" (KJV)

God gave us power; let's rise up and be who He called us to be! God will take care of what we can't control. As for the "enemy", God has given us the power through His Blood to command the "enemy" and his demon minions through our spoken word to flee! So let's get our armor of God on like the Word says and plead that precious, powerful blood all over our homes, cars, bodies, work, and families daily!
You're familiar with the phrase: get your big boy pants on? Well, let's get our Armor of God on!

1 John 4:4 - "You are from God and have overcome them (the enemy), because the one who is in you (Holy Spirit) is greater than the one who is in the world." (KJV)

James 4:7 - "Submit yourselves therefore to God. Resist the devil, an he will flee from you." (KJV)

We can speak to our mountains! We don't have to go around them, we don't have to even climb that thing!

Mark 11:23 - "Say to that mountain, be thrown into the sea and it will happen. <u>But you must believe it will happen and have no doubt in your heart.</u>" (NLT)

The Lord had a reason for her healing, he was about to fill her heart with what had been missing and broken for over 20 years! God brought a Godly man into her life. I count their encounter miraculous even. She had been hurt so before, that trusting a man was super difficult, especially a stranger. So, in God's omnipotent wisdom sent not a stranger.

Isaiah 40:31 - "But they that wait upon the Lord shall renew their strength; They will mount up with wings like eagles, They will run and not get tired, They will walk and not become weary." (KJV)

God allowed them to meet back in 1986. Connie had attended college in Conway (Central Baptist College) before transferring to Jonesboro. She went to CBC only one year, the same year Don was there. He had noticed her as he said most of the male student body had (she was very beautiful). He had wanted to ask her out, but she was dating the man she later married. She had no idea so many were interested in dating her. She was so faithful to him, she would've never dreamed of thinking of someone else even while dating. Almost 26 years later God brought Connie and Don back in contact. Don could relate to Connie's hurt as well and understand it for he had been hurt in the same way. I don't think either were looking or expecting to ever find love again. Turns out, God thought they were ready. God uses all kinds of ways to get the job done, even technology...

Connie was always on the computer either reading or doing social media. She stayed glued to that, especially since she was limited on what she could do. Her computer began to mess up so her best friend, Renee told her to reach out to Don (who is a whiz at computers). She'd probably admit now but I betcha then Renee had an ulterior motive other than fixing Connie's computer. After getting her computer fixed, Don's daughter, Allison began connecting with Connie on social media. It was actually Allison who instigated the first date. One thing led to another and they had their first date here in Conway. Connie was skeptical prior, but was lit from within after. They began dating and Connie seemed so fulfilled and happy, truly happy. Finally, she had someone to love her and be faithful to her! I remember shortly after they started dating, Connie called a meeting with Burns in their secret place (under the staircase). They often met here to whisper about top secret stuff that only aunts and nephews share. She told Burns there that he would soon have an uncle. How do I know that? Well, their secrets never stayed locked long. Burns asked if Don had proposed. Connie said no, but he will, God told me

so. In March of 2012 they married. They had their adjustments to
make as most do but they truly loved each other.

Connie, Don, and the children

Chapter 7
Preparations for Home

Connie and Don were working on their house to try and sell it

so Connie went to Wynne (our parent's home) some so Don could do the renovations. She came to my house about three weeks prior to Thanksgiving 2014 with plans to go on to Wynne after. She stayed two or three nights I think. She was overly sensitive while here. She was nostalgic and seemed so touched by so many things. Colton (Don's eldest son) called her almost daily if she wasn't in Hot Springs (their hometown). She had a voice mail from him and I'll never forget her face as she let me listen to it. He usually started out by saying, "Connie, I looooove you" then would proceed with his message. She came in the kitchen and said, "listen to what I got!". She was so thankful for him and loved him so! I remember her tears too as she re listened to that message several more times. Shortly after that, she was sitting across from me at my bar, I was washing dishes. She was staring at me. I asked, "why are you staring so?!" She got serious and teary and said, "Don't think I'm weird, I just wanted to watch you. You know you have Grandmomma's fingers, Momma's hands, and Mamaw's mouth. I've never noticed those

64

things before." Knowing me, I made light of it and just smiled or laughed it off. But, even through that, I thought something was off. She seemed to be wanting to memorize me almost. While here, we ate out and I took her picture with Burns at the restaurant. I never did that before. She was always the one to say, "take our picture...". I know now why it came over me to do so. After her visit here, she went on to Wynne to stay for a couple of weeks. Momma said while there she was also nostalgic and easy to cry. Connie had been around this her whole life, yet had never been interested in Momma's old jewelry box, to name one thing. She came in and was really examining each piece and asking about it. Momma thought, how odd, you've never been interested in that before and it's always been here.

The last Sunday she was in Wynne, she went to church. She was late because her arms were hurting so that she could barely dry her hair. Connie had been diagnosed with Fibromyalgia and on top of that still suffered tons of side effects from the plethora of prescriptions she had to take. So dressing, especially early in the mornings were often hard. Ivan Parker was singing there that day. She liked him and tried hard to make it. When she walked in, he was just beginning one of her favorite songs, "Beulah Land". She cried so. During the invitation, two ladies had gone to kneel at the alter. Connie left her pew and began to walk forward to the alter. Momma thought she was going to the alter for herself. Going to the alter during the invitation to kneel or to speak to the pastor wasn't something Connie did often if at all so it puzzled Momma a little as to why she was going.

Connie walked with a limp and used a cane ever since her surgery and could not get down on the floor easily, at all frankly. Momma was amazed and just stared at Connie as she walked down that side aisle to the front- straight and with NO limp and without her cane! Momma even at that moment was in awe watching her. Momma called me later that day even and was commenting on how she watched Connie walk so straight, tall and with no limp. Momma was telling me this in tears which I thought odd. She said, "Cameron, I just couldn't keep my eyes off of her, it was like she was someone else, she was different..." I understood her reaction because I'd had a similar one the day she was watching me at the sink. Its very hard to put into words. Now as she still recalls this, she is even more amazed due to the timing etc. Connie wasn't going up for herself. She went to kneel with those two ladies. She prayed with one then the other. My cousin was one and knew of Connie's health and offered to help her up at the end. Strangely, Connie KNELT at that alter with no trouble and got up totally on her own just as smoothly as a child would rise! She said Connie said, "Nope, I'm fine, I can make it fine." How odd all this is!

Why did Connie go up, why did she feel the need to minister to these ladies and more than this how did she walk down and kneel as if her health issues were gone?! I wish I had [When life gets too hard to stand, kneel] been there that day.

Momma recalls so often and will never forget how Connie looked as she walked down and back. She said her face was so bright/happy/

66

peaceful as well. If we were only reflecting and seeing that now you could say we imagined that. But, that day Momma called just to tell me about it and comment on all these things. Momma couldn't understand then why she saw Connie this way and how Connie was able to kneel etc. I remember Momma's voice that day. She cried even while telling me, she was that moved. I remember Momma's words with tears as she said, "...Cameron, I wish you could have seen Connie walk down that aisle this morning! She was walking so straight, so tall, wasn't limping, and didn't need her cane!" She even told me that another relative commented that day after church as well that Connie looked so "different", said she looked so "happy, so at peace!" I remember thinking Momma was really going on about this. And honestly it puzzled me at the time why. Now it's so clear.

At lunch after church Connie noticed someone. She saw the woman who had taken (TAKEN!) her job at Senior Care. Like I mentioned earlier, her health caused her to have to resign. But, there was a "lady"

Psalm 39:4 - "Lord, help me to realize how brief my time on earth will be. Help me to know that I am here for but a moment more." (TLB)

waiting in the wings who could just taste that position and did all she could to report Connie's declining abilities to the ones in charge. She did not behave in a Christ-like manner to put it frankly and to shorten the story. Connie had very hurt/hard feelings toward her all these years. She used to say how she'd love to run into her (and give her a piece of her mind I'm sure). Our town is very small; it was odd

Connie never did run into her all those years. But today, here she was after almost 20 years in the same restaurant with her. Connie told Momma and said, "I'm going over there!" Connie went over with Christ leading the way and spoke not of their history but spoke in love, just love. Connie came back in tears and told Momma and Daddy how glad she was that she had that opportunity. So many preparations were being made! **Preparations! Preparations!** Thinking back to what I mentioned on forgiveness. Oh how hard it is when we are led only by our humanness/our flesh to let go and let God. To let go and forgive. Oh how easy and rewarding it is when we do. Why do we so often insist on doing it the hard way! After all, our *"...spirit is willing, but the flesh is weak." -Matthew 26:41* (KJV)

Connie and Momma went to Jonesboro to shop a couple days after and Connie listened to the Ivan Parker CD that she had bought the previous Sunday all the way there and back. Momma joked and said, you're going to wear that out before you even give it. Connie had bought to give to Don's parents for Christmas. Connie said, "I know, I just can't stop listening to it." Later, we read something on that disk that was odd as well. While in Jonesboro, she and Momma had a great time. While eating, Connie had the waitress take their picture. That is the only picture of just the two of them. We just don't take many pictures unless Burns is there and even then we don't take as many as we should. So thankful Connie thought to do that! We've eaten out countless times of course as have all people, but Momma saved this menu and even wrote their names beside what they ordered. At the time her thoughts were, "lets keep this so we'll remember what we ordered since we liked it so." Now, we see God had a sweeter purpose for saving that "autographed" menu.

"Those who leave everything in God's hand will eventually see God's hand in everything."- unknown author

Later that week, Connie had lunch with a old friend she hadn't seen in years (Kim). Later I found the menu for that lunch as well and strangely Connie had labeled that menu as well with what she ordered.

Connie's cat (aka Connie's child or "Harriet") had been living in Wynne all this time. Don had two dogs and 4 children so Connie couldn't take Harriet there until she figured out how to integrate everyone. Harriet is an extremely introverted and shy/skittish cat. Even to hear the doorbell or a strange voice sends her in hiding for hours. We had begged Connie on numerous occasions to let Harriet live in Wynne permanently. Connie wouldn't hear of it. She knew someday she could take Harriet home to Hot Springs. Yet, the day Connie left for home (on her last trip to Wynne, 2014) she stopped at her car before getting in and called back to Momma, tears streaming down her face and said, "Momma, I realize Harriet needs to live with you". Wow, so not Connie! No one had even mentioned Harriet's living arrangements this trip. **Preparations! Preparations!**

Speaking of preparation, Connie was at her friend Darlene's house close to this time. She said, "I want to go home!" Darlene asked, "which home: Wynne, Conway, Hot Springs...?" Connie answered, "My real home...where my Heavenly Father is!" A Christian always has a desire to go "home". I do. But like Grandaddy always said, "I want to go to heaven, just not today". That wasn't Connie. She said often over the years that she wished Jesus would return that very second. Momma used to say to her she wanted Him to return too, but she also wanted to be here and live a few more years and hopefully live out her life expectancy. Connie had a strange desire to go and soon. She told me years ago that she would never grow old. I probably laughed it off (I can't remember) and thought she meant she wouldn't age (like get gray etc; I took it to mean in a physical way, to age). She said, "I don't mean that; I mean I won't live long enough to be old". What a thing to say, I thought then AND now. Now, it is all so clear.

Preparations! Preparations!

Chapter 8
Just a Little While

December 7, 2014

On December 6, 2014, Connie and Don went to a reunion out of

town. She had a great time seeing old friends. The next day they
went to a church she'd been anxious to visit. Our home church
spoiled us, we both wanted to find that where we live. She and Don
visited many, but she just didn't feel like any were enough like "home".
This Sunday, she thought she had and told Don she wanted to go
back the next Sunday.

That night, the 7th, Don took her to see a 1940's movie showing one
day only. It was one of our family's favorites: "Christmas In

Connecticut". She was ecstatic about going! Don took one picture of her in particular standing in front of the movie poster that I will mention later.

It was a double feature with "Christmas Carol" playing first. She wasn't feeling very well, felt very tired so she dozed during much of the first. She told Don to be sure and wake her for "Christmas in Connecticut"; she wasn't going to miss that! She felt a cold coming on or something, even thought that she may have just over-done-it at the reunion.

The Friday before the reunion, she and her friend Darlene went shopping. She'd wanted a Christmas wreath for their front door and had wanted to go before now, but had some days where she wasn't feeling well so had put it off. They went to Hobby Lobby and spent literally hours picking out things for it. I think it wore Darlene out. Connie had that reputation of taking forever at a store! She called Momma on Monday night and talked forever about that wreath. Momma told me later that she thought she'd have to tell Connie she had to get off because her ear was even hurting; Momma was tickled. Don said Connie told him too about each piece and what each piece stood for. Now here is a way Connie and I are different, I would've picked out a wreath already made or just had a florist make it up for me according to whatever was in style. Not Connie, she wanted that to reflect their life, their family, their story. While they were dating, Connie had gotten Don a snowman plaque with "Terry" on it that said "Let it Snow".

Connie looooooved snow. She was worse than a child when snow would be forecasted. She would get so excited! She'd call Burns to make sure he knew it was forecasted etc. Then they'd call or text each other to see if either one was getting any. So she had a snowman in the center of the wreath and had Darlene make a chalkboard sign that said "Let it Snow". She also had curly pieces on it. That part makes me laugh. She was comical when it came to wrapping gifts. She took forever! I'm trying to think of a word that is more intense than "forever"! Is there one? Forever is such an understatement. She labored so when she wrapped. She'd curl up every strand of her ribbons so tight; she'd pull and pull those strands through those scissors. And she'd have an immense amount of ribbon on each. She'd be at least 30 minutes per package, really. So, there are "curlies" all over her wreath. Momma told me later that night, "Connie just talked and talked, I've never heard of such, we talked longer than I think we ever have". And it was mainly about that wreath. Let me be clear too, this was not a rare conversation, Connie

73

and I both call Momma every day (sometimes multiple times a day) practically, barring something odd and always have. As I will disclose later, this special/long/memorable conversation was the last Momma and Connie were to have.

On Tuesday, the 9th, Connie called me. She said she wasn't feeling very well, had a cold she thought. She wanted me to call Momma and ask her not to call and tell her she wouldn't be calling since she wanted to lay down and try to get rid of the cold, hoping a nap might make her feel better. Don called me later Tuesday asking what I give Burns for a fever, said Connie had a high one. He treated it and later on it broke. Nothing to alarm anyone. Many get colds/fever. It breaks and they move on. He had stayed home from work Tuesday to care for her. He went back Wednesday since her fever had broken. Colton, his oldest son was there Wednesday so Don had him watch Connie and said to call if she got worse. She did, and fast. Colton recognized this rapid decline and called his dad. Fortunately, they had already made a doctor's appointment so they went on to that. Again, she had called me that morning and asked me to tell Momma she'd call later. She didn't want to worry Momma. We both know far too well how "Momma is". Anytime one of us gets sick, even a cold or headache she says "need me to come?". With she and Daddy, we aren't grown women, we are their <u>little</u> girls. So, Connie just didn't want to worry Momma for "just a cold". By the time they got to the doctor's office, the nurse couldn't get a blood pressure and told Don to get her to the ER immediately. The office was in the same lot as the hospital thankfully. Don kept me informed. I decided not to tell

Momma right then until we knew more. Connie had been so ill so often so long that this didn't seem alarming. This just seemed like a cold that had hit her usually hard and something she'd be ok with as soon as they got fluids/antibiotics in her etc, so I just waited. Later, they admitted her and vented her. I felt it was time to tell Momma; not that I thought she was in danger (I NEVER dreamed that!), just thought it was time for her to know. Daddy works until 9pm so he was still at the plant. Momma grabbed her purse and headed to Conway. Don let Connie know and she wrote him a rather insistent note begging him to tell Momma not to come. She thought the tube would be out by morning and didn't want to scare Momma. She knew Momma would think it was dire just by seeing a breathing tube. See, even Connie thought it was just a minor sickness. So, I called Momma and with much persuasion, had her go back home. She did something unlike Momma, she didn't even call Connie, she just went back home. That is NOT like our momma. Later, we were shown by the Lord why. I will cover that later. So, we had planned that she and Daddy would head to Conway the next morning early.

Thursday, the 11th came, Momma and Daddy were leaving around 5 am. Don contacted me again saying Connie begging "No". The tube was still in and Connie just didn't want them scared. So, I call again and begged them to turn back. Looking back now I can't remember if Don kept me posted during the early part of the morning, that time is a bit blurry for me. The call I got at 10 am is not blurry. He had been texting me, this was a voice call. I could barely understand him; he was in tears and simply said "COME"! I felt so strange.

75

Still, I had no thoughts of Connie being as sick as we later discovered her to be. I understood now how sick she must be; but she had been ill many times before and had bounced back so I just thought: well, she's really ill, but she'll be ok in time. I dreaded calling Momma and Daddy. How would I tell them to come and not spare the horses and at the same time not frighten them? God spoke for me. It takes them two hours to get to Conway. Momma still didn't call Connie during that drive to Conway (again, not like Momma! we see now that God closed her mind to calling Connie). It takes another hour and half to get to Hot Springs from my house. Again, Momma didn't call her or even ask me if I thought she should all that way. Like I said, we found out why later. But I want it clear, Momma not calling her since Monday is NOT normal by any means!

When we pulled up at the entrance, Don was there and I could tell something was majorly wrong. No smile, no greetings, just "come quickly, the doctor wants to meet with us". I parked the car and felt such a unrest. I had no idea where to go so I just headed to the ICU. I was trying to find all of them. I walked past Connie's room, looked in and didn't even recognize her so I kept walking! She was so bad and hooked up to so many things you could hardly see her. The nurse found me and took me to the meeting. It was short and direct and we were told to "pray and prepare!" "WHAT?!?!?! What in the world did this doctor mean? Not my sister! She just has a cold!!!! You don't know her, she gets sick a lot and everything even headaches hit her harder than most, she WILL BE FINE, SHE IS FINE"- that is what I was shouting in my head. My parents looked like they had been in

76

an accident. A shock that they never thought they'd be given! I'll never forget their face! We sat in silence probably 5 minutes; it felt like days! Then when we finally found our voice we began telling him he had to be wrong and even if he was right our Lord wouldn't take her! I NEVER thought my sister wouldn't walk out. My ONLY fear was how this was affecting Momma and Daddy! The first walk to see Connie was a long one. We hadn't seen her (at least I thought I hadn't) and we had just heard this unbelievable news from the doctor. We had no idea what to say to her, how to act and yet we said nothing to each other on the way. What could we say, this is where our shock set in.

God gave us a boost of supernatural strength the moment we opened her curtain and her eyes met ours.

> "When God pushes you to the edge, trust Him fully, because only two things can happen. Either He will catch you when you fall or He will teach you how to fly"- author unknown

Those beautiful brown, loving eyes. At this point, they were still bright, alert, and beautiful! When I passed her room earlier and didn't recognize her, it was different now. This time, the Lord was easing my mind. This time I didn't just see the ventilator, the tubes, etc; I just saw THOSE EYES! I said something comical/sarcastic to her the way we always do to each other and smiled. She of course couldn't talk but she rolled those eyes the way we always do as if to say, "you little stinker!" Same ole Connie. That was very short lived.

77

We know now the Lord just saved that moment for us; the last glimpse of "Connie" we'd ever see on this earth, literally the last. It was literally seconds after that she was unresponsive and headed down hill faster than one could imagine!

Burns was the light of her life. He didn't go with me; he was with a friend. The Lord had the little boy's mother call me and asked if I thought Burns could talk to his "Aunt Connie". I am so thankful for that call! I put him on speaker and he talked to "Aunt Connie". That was one of the last times she showed any life in her eyes, reactions. The last time was later that night when I showed her Burns' picture (the one I had taken before Thanksgiving, the two of them together). I moved it side to side to test her eyes and she moved her eyes with. No other time after could we get a reaction of any kind, that is how fast she plummeted!

A dear friend of mine came and stayed with us the entire time. She explained later that she couldn't leave because the Lord had revealed to her that Connie would not make it. After that revelation, the Lord told her to tell me to share anything I wanted to or needed to, to Connie. I remember going in the waiting room and hearing those words come from her mouth. I was mixed, I thought: what is she thinking?! Connie is going to be FINE! But at the same time I felt a feeling from the Holy Spirit that said, "don't ignore this, take heed to what she says".

She knows loss all too well, she had lost her youngest son just two years prior, he was only 12. I can't think of anyone more appropriate to be with us during that time.   She alone could understand what Momma and Daddy were about to feel/face.

Regardless of what we witnessed or what the doctor warned, we never dreamed it would happen. We prayed over her over and over. Momma, Daddy, and I held her hands, rubbed her feet just about the entire 24 hours. We sang songs Momma and Grandmomma sang to us as they rocked us when we were little. We sang favorite old hymns too. We sang until we were hardly able to sing any more. The nurses stopped us some because they said she just needed quiet. Each time they asked us to step out so they could check her etc we would see a decline and they would say "now this organ is failing/has failed". That's how fast it went. That night was horrible. No more response from Connie. Nothing we said or did, no touch caused a reaction. When I say we could see a decline each time we left the room, that was literal. Her physical appearance was constantly changing, still we couldn't accept what we were being told. Earlier in the night they were concerned about her kidneys not functioning and that causing poison to build up. I remembered when we were little, Momma running the water to get us to use the bathroom when we had trouble. I wanted my sister well! I wanted a miracle! I went to that faucet and ran the water and begged Connie to try! "Connie, listen to the water, hear it? Try, try to go, please try, listen to the water, hear the water...", I pleaded. On and on I tried with the tears flowing down my face. Nothing worked! Once her fever spiked so high they covered her body entirely and hooked up a portable AC unit to her bed, she was like ice. We prayed and the fever broke, we were so hopeful! Next the fever dropped dangerously low and they began heating her body with all kinds of heated blankets. Again we prayed, we were so hopeful! Her fever finally normalized. Again we had hope and thought things would turn. Although I didn't admit to Momma, Daddy, Don, or myself even, there was a time the nurse came in, that deep down I must have known. She shown a light in Connie's eyes and I could sense hurt in the nurse's body language. I got up and insisted she tell me what was wrong with Connie's eyes. She said, "no, honey you don't want to see". I crying said, "yes I do!". She showed me and then I think I must have known, Connie's beautiful eyes were gone, replaced by something I didn't recognize. Her liver had failed by this time and had caused her eyes to... die almost for lack of better term. Things like this went on all through that long night. Again, when life gets too hard to stand...KNEEL! And

this is what I did, I knelt on that floor many times begging the Lord, "Don't take my sister, Father, NO!" Over and over I did this. Over and over we prayed at her bedside. What was going on?! This can't be! Was this the girl just a short while ago was kneeling at the alter of Caldwell Baptist looking and feeling more alive than ever in her life, and here I am kneeling in a hospital room begging for her life! This is a dream, surely I'll wake and say to Connie, "you won't believe what I dreamed"; she'd laugh and say, "mercy, what did you eat for supper last night". "Father, NO!"

On Friday, the 12th, the doctor told us in a meeting that the time was drawing short. He asked us to decide if she should be resuscitated in

80

case her heart failed. What?! I still couldn't face this! Was I dreaming?! I thought, "I don't know this doctor, I wish I could ask Dr. Tilley (my doctor and someone I trust; he's a Godly man first and foremost) but how can I reach him?! Its almost closing time, its Friday, they wouldn't let me talk to him anyway right now (since when you try to reach a physician you always have to leave a message etc). Lord, help us!" The doctor warned it could be soon, that day or the next and really any moment in between.

Chapter 9
Father, No!

As we walked back to her room, my phone rang. Here is where

the series of *Connie's Miracles* begins:

It was him!! It was DR TILLEY!!! See, my husband had been ill. We had been told Dr. Tilley's office would call him that Monday, the 8th with some news we needed. They didn't and we wondered why since they are always so prompt. Another strange thing is we didn't call them Tuesday or Wednesday ourselves to find out. Actually, my husband had asked if I would call late Monday and I said, "No, they'll call". So not like me to wait like that. For that matter, so not like Dr. Tilley's office to forget or neglect to call. When I answered, Brad (Dr. Tilley) started in by apologizing for the delay. Let me explain this as well: the office, not Brad, was to call Monday and not me, my husband. So, Brad is headed out to go hunting and it comes to his mind to ask and his staff said they hadn't called yet. So, he decides to call on his own and he just has MY number!!!!! I quickly interrupted him and started filling him in on Connie and what we'd just been told.

He didn't hesitate and said, "No, under no circumstances allow them to do artificial resuscitation on her!" I quickly hung up and felt the urgency (from the Holy Spirit) to RUN to Connie's room. I had been given no word from the staff that she was worse, I just felt that urgency so putting my inhibitions aside I began running down the hall. As I approached the room, I could hear Momma crying from down the hall. I couldn't see Connie at this point, but I knew something was happening. I just yelled at Momma, "Tell them to stop, Dr. Tilley said NO!". By now I was in and the nurses were laying Connie back down gently. Momma filled me in as to what took place while I was on the phone with Brad: she and Daddy went on back to Connie's room after the meeting, I had stayed behind to answer my phone. When they got to Connie's room, it happened-what the doctor had just tried to prepare us for now was happening. Her heart was failing. Since no one from the family had made a decision yet, the nurses were alone and were going to start the artificial resuscitation. When Momma arrived, they had the equipment hooked up and had Connie in position; that is when I yelled to Momma. It's hard to convey sometimes in words exactly what took place in any event. I hope I convey the time frame adequately here. All these events took place in direct sequence and one right after the other, just boom, boom, boom. Not even seconds in between.

We knew then that the end was near. For the first time, we began seeing things as they were, as the doctor tried to prepare us for. Momma wouldn't let go of Connie's hand. We had had no response

83

from Connie for several hours, not since the day before. No longer could she "talk" to us with her eyes, no longer would she grab our hands or move her foot. Her eyes were not "Connie", they were almost as if she had already gone. I had refused to admit my sister would leave us. Now, I felt the reality of the message my dear friend had tried to tell me earlier. She had tried to warn me. Later she revealed that God had told her Connie would be going "home". I felt that urgency now as well. I left Connie's side and knelt on the floor again begging the Lord to not take my sister. All I could say was, "Jesus, please don't take my sister!". Over and over again I begged Him. While I knelt the nurse told Momma it was almost over, Connie was going. I couldn't get up, I still kept begging. Later, I went to Connie and begged her to ask Jesus to let her come back, to ask Him to let her stay! I knew, I just knew she'd seen the Father, she was on her way! Looking back now, I'm ashamed I asked her such. How could I ask her that if I loved her?! To leave Jesus! Who would do such a thing?! The nurse said Connie needed to go, it was time. There was nothing left to keep her alive. The nurse asked Momma to tell Connie that (the nurse was a believer). The nurse said, "I don't think she'll go until you give her permission, Momma". Momma then whispered to Connie:

"Connie, run to Jesus, run to Him, its ok to go"! Daddy then said in the same sweet/calm voice I've heard my whole life: "Daddy loves the shug" ("Shug" was one of many nicknames Daddy had for Connie). He didn't sound desperate, he didn't sound alarmed. To her it must

84

have sounded like all the times before. So, when she needed him the most and for the final time, he was still "Daddy".

"It's not the load that breaks you down. Its the way you carry it."- C.S. Lewis

Matthew 11:29,30 - "Take my yoke upon you...and ye shall find rest..for my yoke is easy and my burden is light." (KJV)

Momma, Daddy, and Connie

At that moment the monitor flat lined and they pronounced her gone. "They" pronounced her isn't quite accurate. The doctor wasn't in there. The head nurse was the one that instructed Momma, but the one that pronounced Connie gone was only seen by Momma. I can't explain it any better. Momma said that she was a lady she'd never seen and wasn't even in the room during the final stages; she was just there to say, "Momma, she's gone". Being "new" to us, how did she know we call Momma, "Momma". Who was this woman? I don't know. I'm not going to add something that didn't take place. After you read the rest of this story maybe you can determine for yourself who this woman was. To us, it was the 2nd unusual/hard to explain in earthly terms events that led to many.

Its easy for us to sit here and try to make a story sound more "spiritual" or more eventful. I don't think that was the case. I tried extremely hard to write just as it happened. Miracles are just that, miracles, they don't need punching up to sound more "believable". Sometimes they aren't believable except to those who see them with their own eyes.

Back to what Momma said to Connie at the end: I truly feel the Lord had Connie in His presence then and allowed my momma (her caregiver for 48 years) to give her permission once again when Momma said, "Connie, run to Jesus...". Is that just my opinion? Of course, but I believe the Lord truly understands the depth of a mother's heart/love because, after all, who but God designed a mother's heart. He thought of Mary first of all and made sure she

86

would be cared for and comforted after His crucifixion. He knew His mother would be experiencing great pain over losing her child. He loves my momma too and I feel He allowed her to be "Momma" one last time. As you read on you will see the rest of *Connie's Miracles* unfold.

For quite a while, I struggled with my own faith. I couldn't understand why God took my sister while we were praying for and expecting a healing. I went on a 2 year study/journey which ended just recently actually related to my struggle. At first I thought it was her time regardless, period. The Holy Spirit kept prompting me to dig deeper. The enemy attacked and made me feel perhaps I lacked the faith needed to save her life. Then he attacked making me feel my lack of knowledge on how to pray for healing was the cause. (1 Peter 2:24 says that by His stripes we <u>were</u> healed. The focus there being "were" which means He healed us on the cross and we but have to receive it.) As earlier mentioned in the story, I know God didn't intend anyone to be ill and intends all to be well so I became very confused and therefore the enemy saw a weak spot and began having a hay day with me. This was a long hard journey. Many times I ended up with my face in the carpet weeping, blaming myself in all kinds of ways. After much prayer and reading the Word I came to the end of the journey. The Holy Spirit revealed to me that our words are powerful. There are countless Scriptures regarding this, I'll list a couple:

Proverbs 18:21 - "Death and life are in the power of the tongue; and they that love it shall eat the fruit thereof." (KJV) The Living Bible says it more bluntly: *"Those who love to talk will suffer the consequences. Men have died for saying the wrong thing."*

Mark 11:23 - "...whosoever shall say to this mountain, Be thou removed, and be thou cast into the sea; and shall not doubt in his heart, but shall believe that those things which he saith shall come to pass; he shall have whatever he saith." (KJV)

Wow, we could stop there I believe. There are many more though. Its a study all believers should dig into. The spoken word can receive salvation, can heal, can express love, can through Jesus' name cast out devils, rebuke the enemy... At the same time can curse, cause doubt and unbelief upon ourselves and others, can allow the enemy a foothold... I've settled on the fact that will shock and possibly disturb and even anger some: God didn't call Connie home, instead He received her home. It did not take God by surprise however. He knew before she was conceived how long she would live- how many seconds even, how many and what would occur during each. As such, He allowed such preparation from her. I believe her spoken words of "I'll not grow old, I am ready to go home, I want to go home"...

I heard a message recently on this very thing. A family who had lost a loved one asked the pastor: we prayed, we believed for healing, why?! The pastor said in these cases, the prayer of the individual supersedes any others prayers. I don't know what Connie was praying for during this time but I firmly believe based on the outcome she was asking to go on home to which she'd desired so often. God honored that and so lovingly received her. I'll go a step farther and say I firmly believe had Connie asked for healing and believed for it, God would've honored that request equally. I take the Scripture literally and am reminded now of *"ask and it shall be given unto you..." Matthew 7*

Another truth I discovered was I did not need to beg my Jesus for my sister's life or anything. Faith does not beg. Seeking God and crying out for Him to work in our life is different from begging. One knows that God can and ultimately will work, the other is fearful that He will not work and is pleading for Him to change His mind. Seeking God shows perseverance and has faith at its core. Begging has a measure of fear laced with manipulation within it. We *beg* to someone who may be indifferent to our situation and <u>may</u> be able to help; we *seek* someone who cares and <u>is </u>capable to help. *James 1:6,7: "But when he asks, he must believe and not doubt, because he who doubts is like a wave of the sea, blown and tossed by the wind. That man should not think he will receive anything from the*

Lord; he is a double-minded man, unstable in all he does." (NIV)

Philippians 4:6 tells us to be anxious for nothing. 1 John 5:14 tells us to be confident in the fact that whatever we ask of Him, if we pray according to His Will, He hears and thereby grants the requests we have asked of Him. He is a loving Father. A loving earthly father takes no pleasure in his children begging. How much more does our Heavenly Father love us?

Persistency, yes; begging, no. As in the parable told in Luke 18 regarding the woman persistently insisting that the unjust judge avenge her. Prayer is about faith. As in Hebrews 11:6, we are to diligently seek Him. As in Luke 11:9 ask and it shall be given you; seek and ye shall find; knock and it shall be opened unto you. The parable in the verses preceding this spoke of a man asking a neighbor in the late hour of the night for food. He kept knocking, he didn't give up and go to the next neighbor. When we pray and don't receive an immediate answer (our time table), we aren't to think God expects us to begin begging or yelling louder, or worse yet, find another way. By staying at God's door (throne) knocking we are showing faith because we believe there isn't another door that has what we need/has the answer. God is our only source. This truth is not just for crisis moments, its for everyday occurrences. So let's keep on knocking, keep on leaning, keep on expecting; for God is awake, He's alert, He's willing, and He's able.

Chapter 10
In His Presence

We were then asked to leave the room while they removed

everything Connie had been using to stay alive. When we saw
Connie next I almost fell to the ground. Her face glowed from her
forehead down! Before I could even say it, Momma shouted the
same! I guess its safe to say we all lost our inhibitions while at the
hospital. We had so much to be emotional, and at this point
overwhelmingly excited about, we didn't care who heard us. We then
saw something else, her wrinkles were gone, all of them! She had the
face of a woman, yes, but the complexion of a child! Connie had lost
too much weight too quickly in the months preceding her illness.
She had began to wrinkle more than she probably should have. We
had kidded her just months before saying she better change her
moisturizer etc. She would tease me about my graying hair and I
would tease her about her wrinkles. But now, these were GONE!
How is this possible?! Momma then noticed her mouth. It was so
sweet! She said, it looks like when she was little! I'll never forget that

face, that beautiful, glowing, heaven-seen face! Momma termed it: "A Radiant Glow". Later, I told a dear friend of mine and she said, "A radiant glow as if reflecting her Savior's presence in front of her!" I've heard of this before- people seeing their loved one's face "glowing". Can you imagine what Connie saw or any <u>believer</u> after they take their last breath?! Scripture records how Moses' appearance changed when He was in the presence of God: *Exodus 34:35 - "...they saw that his face was radiant..."*

So sweet and precious was the area around her mouth; just as when she was little. Later when we were choosing pictures for her home-going service slideshow we ran across that particular picture. From her nose down it was as is here! Dimples, precious expression, rosy glow and all.

There we were with her, just couldn't stop looking at her face! Glowing, no wrinkles, and that sweet smile/mouth!

As I mentioned earlier, Momma had held Connie's hand almost the entire time. By now of course, Connie was gone and Momma couldn't break the grip. That was so hard to see. Momma wept and wept saying, "She won't let go! She won't let go! I can't let go! I can't! I don't want to let go!" Can you imagine how she felt as a mother knowing she'd never see/hold that hand again on this earth?! My heart couldn't hardly take it. I love my momma so and to see this immense pain that I had no control to remove.

After the funeral home prepared her, we noticed the wrinkles were back. Momma said, "that's because Connie isn't in this shell, this is just a shell, SHE is with the Father and He is no longer caring for this shell!" I loved that! I believe that is true! Some believe angels come for us, some believe Jesus. Regardless of who comes, can you imagine?! Burns even said, "Momma, I think God rewarded Grandmomma Myrtle and Grandaddy Homer by letting them come get Aunt Connie." I loved that thought too! Regardless, wasn't that entry into heaven glorious, amazing, beyond words?! To see the Savior! How thankful we are, beyond words that Connie recognized at the age of 29 that she was not saved and took care of that! So many times adults are too ashamed for whatever reason to admit that and maybe never make that right. Had that been Connie's case, it wouldn't have mattered how we prayed for her or how we'd "hoped" her into heaven. No one can save you. Boy, if that were possible we certainly could have gotten a free pass, if you will, from our grandparents or parents as would some of you I imagine. Each person has to stand before the Father alone and each person has to ask Jesus into their hearts alone.

We hurt so terribly, but we have our moments of great joy also because we know where Connie is beyond a shadow of a doubt and we know because we are saved that we WILL see her again. I'm so thankful we don't have to just "hope" that. We KNOW it! We know she IS WITH THE FATHER, whole, and completely healed!

Some believe that when a person dies, they just sleep in the grave until the rapture of the church, the resurrection. I can't rely on what preachers tell me, what books say, what the latest craze on Facebook is sharing. I have to base ALL my feelings, beliefs, convictions on what I read in the Bible. What comes to mind immediately is when the thief died on the cross. Jesus said to him: *"Truly I tell you, today you will be with me in paradise." - John 23:43* (KJV) He didn't say, today you will sleep well my friend and one day we'll be together! 2 Corinthians 5:8 speaks of being absent from the body and present with the Lord. I could write another page or more about this, but to me these verses settle that argument for me.

Many well meaning pastors and teachers take verses and attach to others to come up with a puzzle of phrases that seem to jive, seem to teach a doctrine. John 23:43 all alone substantiates our destination. I've even heard those who think when someone dies no one comes for them, their souls and bodies are just waiting for the day of the Lord and as a whole go to the grave. Connie was the first and only person I have ever been with when they left this earth. Her face, her

94

glow, her smile was not a reaction from heading to nothingness, to years of sleep... I of course do not know who came for Connie. Was it an angel, was it Jesus, was it our grandparents even; I do believe someone did. I also believe that confusion about doctrine is from the devil. He uses whatever means he can to confuse new believers, change minds of seasoned ones, and distract non believers through this confusion which can lead to division and tragically a lost state. This distraction is to turn our heads from the cross which is a clear cut doctrine. If the enemy can distract from the cross, he wins, for it is only through the cross we can come to the Savior. The above debate of course isn't the only one. There are those that would argue with you all the way from Genesis to Revelation and back. If you are reading this and disagreeing with me on some points that is your right. Let us as believers always have our eyes on the cross and not fall into the temptation of arguing someone away from it.

Connie had said that at her home-going service she would want the plan of salvation explained. I'm not sure why she would even talk about her funeral. I don't think I ever have unless to her when she did. We used to say what songs we'd like but Connie would talk in detail about her funeral. She must have had a sense from the Lord and/or an immense urge to go home (which she did) that's the only way I can explain it. She certainly seemed to have a sense the weeks leading up to this. But, I certainly don't think she thought her time was this close. God was preparing her unbeknownst to her.

At someone's funeral service, certainly you can speak of the one who has passed away and we did Connie, but it's too late for them. Their fate is sealed. Connie understood that and knew there is always someone who hasn't accepted Jesus as their Savior at a funeral. We made sure the plan of salvation was explained. What a glorious thing if someone had come to know Him while there! If you are reading this and are totally in the dark about "salvation" or maybe you're like Connie and thought you were saved or maybe you're just plain lost and know it– you can get this settled right now. Maybe you've never been in a church or around Christians and you don't even know what the words "saved" and "lost" mean. You can get your eternity settled today. I will explain this as if you are one that has never heard this before. Jesus is God's Son. He came to this earth more than 2,000 years ago. His purpose for coming was to die on the cross for us. He was crucified for you and me. He was buried, but He is NOT dead! After 3 days He rose again! He conquered death! We have 2 choices only. Some say we have many, not so, we have two. One is to believe in Jesus, one is to not. Simply, if you do not accept Jesus into your heart you will go to hell when you die. There are no second chances. To be "saved" all you have to do is admit that you are a sinner (we all are) and ask Jesus to forgive you and come into your heart and believe He is the Son of God. The only path to salvation. Then start reading the Bible, studying it. Find a church that preaches the Bible. Pray about the church you should go to. Sadly, there are many that do not preach the truth. Grow in the Lord, try to learn all you can about Him. Number one is pray! Pray! PRAY! Just as important as prayer is, read your Bible! Sadly, today especially, there are so many who claim to be Christians and are just trying to deceive and make

Christians weak. Become a part of a church that accepts you as you are but doesn't leave you like that, steps on your toes, teaches faith, preaches against sin (teaches what sin is) and preaches the truth (doesn't add to or take away from the Word) is #1 hard to find and #2 so important to find and be a part of. I myself had to leave our church after 15 years because I felt it wasn't doing that. We visited many and most of all prayed that God would lead us to the right one. I know I got off on a whole other subject but I feel Connie would want this said for sure and I'm going to honor her!

2 Timothy 4:3 - For a time is coming when people will no longer listen to sound and wholesome teaching. They will follow their own desires and will look for preachers who will tell them whatever their itching ears want to hear." (NLT)

Time was short for Connie. None of us are promised another day, another hour.

Also, if you are still a little confused, please reach out to someone and get some help. Don't let this day pass even until you find out how to be saved. You can contact me and I'd be glad to help you. And it doesn't matter how bad you are or how bad your life is. The devil will try and tell you that you have done too much, you're doing too much and there's no way God would ever forgive you or accept you. Don't listen to that lie! It matters not what you're addicted to, how you're living, who you're living with; you may be even serving time. God has saved the hardest of criminals, the evilest of men. Remember

Paul in the Bible, the great man of God? Before he was saved he persecuted Christians! God saved him, changed him, and used him like no other. No one is beyond salvation. After you ask Jesus in your heart, its time to learn how to live like He intends. Being a Christian is not a license to continue in sin. Whatever you did before, whatever life you lived, you are now a new creation, no longer a old sinner. You can now call yourself a saint, the redeemed, a child of God, an heir to the Kingdom, royalty, the seed of Abraham.... You leave behind that old sinner's lifestyle etc. *"Go and sin no more"* – *John 8:11.* (KJV)

Does that mean we become perfect? I wish, don't you? We sure need to strive for that goal though and do the very best we can. When we do fail Him, repent and turn from it and begin again trying again. You'll find that your old ways soon nearly make you sick. Some things may be harder to overcome than others. That's OK, keep on praying, keep praising God for releasing you from those urges (yes, even if the urges are still there), seek a Godly mentor to help you, and learn to read the Bible (ask the Holy Spirit each time you open the Word to show you what to read and for understanding/revelation).

"God help each person who is reading this now and give them guidance as they need it. Amen." - one believer to another

Chapter 11
All Creatures Great and Small

Harriett

*I*left the hospital with Don to go to the house to get Connie's

clothing for the funeral. Wow, how hard to drive up that driveway
and not see her standing at the door, excitingly waiting and waving to
Burns. And to know I never would again. Never had I been to their
home without her.

Don had two dogs as I mentioned earlier. Both took to Connie right
away. Don's parents labeled Connie early on "Pet Whisperer". There
wasn't a animal that didn't take to Connie or visa versa. One of Don's

dogs, "Brownie" especially took to Connie right away. She was a rescue dog, she'd been abused by her previous owner. She feared everyone just about. Momma could usually get a dog/cat to like her, but she never did win Brownie over, very hard cookie indeed. Each time we went to Connie's, Brownie would be near Connie, but be cowered down in fear from us and you could forget petting her. This day was different. I walked in and Brownie came right up to me and rubbed against my leg! I must admit, it took my mind off of my loss for a second. I was that amazed. I went to Connie's bedroom to help Don. Don had a phone call to make. I looked and Brownie was on the bed staring at me. Don't laugh, I felt like I needed to tell her about Connie. So, I knelt down and began telling her. I wish I could've recorded her because words will never convey what I saw. She was listening to me as intently as an adult would, a grieving adult at that. That dog was grieving! She had tears, she had that look that all have (humans) when grieving. I got interrupted during that and had to stop. She'd moved toward the head of the bed by this time. I knelt down again to continue telling her what had happened to her Connie. She scooted herself back to me and rested her head on me and listened once more. I've been around animals all my life and I've never heard/seen such. Don can attest to how she's grieved since. Several months later (in April I think), Don drove up the driveway in Connie's car. Brownie saw it and began yelping out and prancing around the room in joy- she thought it was Connie!

That first night (the 12th) was very hard. I don't think any of us understood the loss we'd suffered and how the future would be

100

without her. Momma began struggling with the fact she'd not called Connie since Monday the 8th. This tore at her so. She said, "Why! Why didn't I call her! Why didn't I check on her! She must have thought I didn't care! She must have thought she was alone, that I'd abandoned her, that her "momma" wasn't there!" All the normal things a loving mother would think. At 4am she was told by the Lord why.

#1 the Lord wanted her last memory to be a great one, the last conversation they had was long/happy/memorable and full of nothing, nothing but hearing Connie be joyful.

#2 Had momma called while Connie had the tube down her throat: Connie couldn't talk back, Momma would've gotten upset, Connie would've sensed that. It would have been too hard on Connie and maybe hard enough (seeing how fragile she was) to have taken her then and it goes without saying that Momma would have felt her call took her- that she was the cause.

God cares about every aspect of our lives, every one! Nothing happened during this time that God didn't orchestrate to His Glory, in His perfect timing. God knew on the 8th that this would be their last phone call. He knew on the day He formed Connie, 48 years ago! He knew all these steps she would take and us. December 12th caught *us* by surprise but not Him! How that knowledge reassures us daily! I say, reassures, I really mean gets us through each day. Loss is natural. Everyone experiences it eventually. To us, Connie's was unnatural, untimely, too soon in our terms. Had we lost her in her 80's for example, would I be writing this, doubtful. We are only human and in our weak moments yes we questioned God, even (and I hate to admit this) were angry with Him. At those times, we just have/had to buckle up, wise up, and pray up. We know that He knew the year, month, day, hour, and second Connie would leave this earth. I realize I may be writing this to others who have lost a child or a family member earlier than "normal". Everyone is different and everyone handles loss differently. We've also learned to be more sensitive to others, not just through their loss but through any hurt they are experiencing. Sometimes, the best way to live with your grief is to minister to someone else. We've also learned to have "grace for the ignorant". People sometimes have good intentions, yet say the (pardon me) stupidest things. I'm sure I've said the same in the past thinking I was helping and having no clue what to say. Momma and Daddy still have a hard time going to church. I do as well when I go there. Memories flood from when we were little, I see her casket at the front, songs are sung that make us think of her... There are many who say, you've grieved enough its time to move on. That is a book in itself that could be written in a hundred different ways from a hundred different viewpoints. I'm no psychologist, I'm not trained as a counselor so I'm not qualified to tell you or anyone else how they should feel. I'm wondering if the qualified ones even can. Living through loss isn't a textbook case, there are too many factors, too many variables. We have to be careful even talking about Connie to some because if our tears come they are quick to judge, if not verbally with their body language. We can't help our tears. I heard someone say who had lost a daughter that after a while they knew they were in a new place in their grieving when they could now think of her and laugh, yet by no means had they stopped the tears. I realize I'm jumping ahead a bit with all this but when the Lord gives me the words I just write them wherever He "interrupted" me to put them even though I'm sure I'm breaking some writing laws.

We do laugh a great deal about Connie now as we remember certain things. But, the tears come quickly too. If they never stop that's ok too. The fact that we can laugh and can in our best ability accept God's Will has put us in a place that we can move on and take one day at a time rejoicing in the blessings we still have.

Galatians 6:2 - "Bear one another's burdens, and so fulfill the law of Christ." (ESV)

Back to those first hours and days:

the way my home is, I can hear Momma and Daddy in their room from my entry. I'll never forget hearing them weep and cry out to the Lord that first morning. I went to their room and there they lay holding hands just broken, broken. That is a sight no child wants to see- their parent's heart literally breaking! I'm hurting, but the loss of a child can't be felt by anyone like a parent.

Psalm 34:18 - "The Lord is close to the brokenhearted and saves those who are crushed in spirit" (NIV)

John 11:35 - "Jesus wept."
That's a verse that people overlook or use as a verse they claim as memorizing to say they know a verse... I think this verse is one of the most powerful in the Word. It wasn't just words amid a sentence. It is a verse all by itself, 2 words. Jesus was grieving for the loss of his friend and grieving for the sisters. There's a verse for anything we are going through today and its just as relevant today as it was 2,000 years ago.

John 11:38 - "Jesus therefore again groaning in himself cometh to the grave..." (KJV)
Jesus understands grieving to the point of groaning as if your own heart is being cut. He is tenderhearted and sees every tear and hurts with us and for us. There is no callousness in my Jesus' hands/heart.

The night before the home-going service we all went back to my parent's home. Harriet, Connie's cat is skittish as I mentioned earlier. She's comfortable with me and Burns, but it ends there other than my parents of course. Yet tonight, she was a different cat, super loving and engaged, even playing with us. She had never been this way before. It was as if Connie had told her (now that she could) to love everyone and to trust us. She continues to be a different cat. After the funeral we all came back to Conway for the week. We brought Harriet. She was also always terrified to ride in a car. Here she was traveling at night (which she had never) in a strange car filled with people, yet she rode so calmly. She had never been to my house so we weren't sure how she would do. She did great! She walked in and acted as if she were home. Don came the next day and stayed a while. She had been terrified of him! I shouldn't tell this but I will-The first time he came to Wynne, Connie was holding Harriet and *attempted* to introduce them. Harriet was so frightened she used the bathroom on Connie! But, here in Conway Harriet walked right up to Don and licked his hand!!!! Boy, Connie must have really given her a talk!

I want to add here, albeit happened much later (10/11/16) another unique, miraculous story about Connie's Harriet. Harriet was a different cat after Connie left as I said, much more at ease. But she was different in another way as well, she missed Connie terribly. How do we know that? That's an impossible one to describe really without living with her and observing her behavior. Not too many months after Connie passed, Harriet became deathly ill. She spent 9 days at

the vet's. We believe she'd given up and wanted to go on. Momma
wasn't ready to let her go and had the vet try everything to help her.
Harriet was the last tangible, living connection to Connie. She did
get better and was able to come home, but she was never to be well
again like before. She was on a downhill slope for sure but slowly. On
October 11, 2016 (Connie's birthday) Harriet was acting very peculiar.
She had set routines that she followed every day and didn't veer from;
today she didn't do any of them. Instead, she laid on the love seat in
the living room where she never laid (yet this was Connie's spot) with
a look on her face that Momma described as "I'm ready, I'm ready to
go to Connie now". There that cat sat for hours without budging for
food, attention, anything. This went on for most of the day. Momma
called me and was almost sure Harriet would pass this day. She didn't
though. Momma still had a feeling her day was soon. Harriet
enjoyed going outside and even that was habitual, she didn't veer
from that route/routine (always in the front yard, always on or close
by the porch). This day, instead of her regular route, she went to a
spot in the yard she'd never gone to before (the backyard, under the
bird house, in view of Connie's window) and just laid there for hours.
Momma felt it best to let her and leave her alone.

The next day she did go, she got to go to her Connie. We buried her
in that very spot (that we believe she chose) in the yard that she had
"marked" just the day before.

Chapter 12
Faith No More

*I*t was now time to prepare for the funeral. When choosing the

casket, all chose the same without telling the other. It was Connie. It was race car red, very unconventional, but that was Connie! Don didn't want her to have a sad/sullen funeral. He wanted her life celebrated. We wanted Connie to shine so others would know the Connie we knew. Don had Darlene make the wreath that Connie had picked out just days before.

He wanted that as her casket arrangement. He brought it in to show us and was able to tell what each piece represented. Each piece Connie had chosen for a reason.

When we arrived at the church we met early with Bro. Jolly. Momma had asked me to arrange Connie's table in the foyer. The visitation started at 9:30, we met with Bro. Jolly at 9. I sat in that meeting totally forgetting that table. Nothing had been laid out! I wasn't even sure where the items were we had brought for it. People had already started to arrive and it hit me: THE TABLE!!! I ran to the church foyer to start. There I was laying this stuff out and people were filing in. I was so embarrassed! I thought: I let Connie down, people will think what in the world is she doing? Why wasn't this done earlier? ETC! I felt like crawling in a hole! While I was there, time got away and I didn't realize it was past time for the visitation to start. Also, I was so overcome with this embarrassment not to mention the emotional roller coaster I was on anyway that I didn't realize a rather obvious conundrum:

<u>Connie wasn't here!</u>

Connie had a reputation for being late, late to everything! Late doing things, late getting to things, late buying gifts, you name it! And I mean LATE! Those that know her realize my emphasis on this. I'm not exaggerating. The girl was always LATE, have I said it enough? About that time, Bro. Jolly made the announcement: "I've just been told the funeral car has been delayed, Connie is going to be LATE". I'm reserved by nature and few have heard me speak loudly. I lost all my inhibitions and yelled out crying in addition saying how appropriate it was that Connie was late to her own funeral! I wonder now if the phrase: "they'll even be late to their own funeral" will now have to be done away with since now someone has! I wonder how many have been late to their own funerals? We need to research that! The fact that there's a well known saying about it would indicate to me that there haven't been many if any. How amazing that the Lord would allow such! I told everyone I could see Connie in heaven laughing that sneaky laugh she had at the humor in this! We counted this as another *Connie Miracle!*

I'm getting a bit ahead in the story but, as I said, I felt so embarrassed about forgetting her table. I struggled with that for a long time. Momma and I discussed it often. On May 25, 2015, I brought it up to Momma once again. She began reassuring me as she always has. Momma's voice became almost silent to me and in my head as clear as a bell I heard Connie! She said, "You need to drop that, I wanted it that way, I wanted people to know 'MY SISTER' did my table and I wanted it to be late!" I could see her saying it with the smirk she and I always used when we were joking with each other. Well, that did it! I've not fretted over that since!

John 14:27 - "I am leaving you with a gift- peace of mind and heart. And the peace I give is a gift the world can't give. So don't be troubled or afraid." (NLT)

Proverbs 12:25 - "Heaviness in the heart of man maketh it stoop; but a good word maketh it glad." (KJV)

Thank you Lord, for caring about my "stooped" spirit and lifting me up!

Her service was the best one I've ever heard! Her best friend, Renee even told me recently, "Cameron, I hope you don't take this wrong, but I enjoyed that funeral!" I completely understood what she meant because even though I was broken, I did too. Bro. Jolly told us in the meeting he was doing Connie's differently than he had ever before. Why? We're not sure. That man has preached hundreds of funerals, why Connie? He said he was going to begin by saying, "Connie lost her faith...she no longer needs it!" And the rest of the message was as unique as that. Our childhood pastor, Bro. Rodney also spoke. We wish we had an audio recording of. We had many say they'd never heard a funeral like that. The most astonishing was the funeral director's reaction. He's seen more funerals than any one and he said that! It was as if Connie had written it. One thing said by Bro. Rodney was meant for me. When we were little, I always thought I was in the way. I felt I was the annoying little sister who pestered her big sister too much. Looking back, I know I did. I looked up to Connie so much, I wanted to be anywhere she was, doing anything she did. We became friends as adults but I often wondered about when we were little. I wondered even as an adult if she wanted me around at all when little, if she wished she'd been an only child. Bro. Rodney was our pastor over 30 years ago. That's a little while ago, right? Well, during the funeral, he recalled an incident when Connie and I were little. The memory he recalled was not earth shattering at all. Why would a preacher hang on to that for almost 40 years. It was so <u>insignificant</u> to him or anyone else. But it was **mountainous** to...

ME!

It was something too small for him to recall and I'm surprised he thought noteworthy to mention this day. Yet, it was just what I needed to hear! And God stored that in Bro. Rodney's memory bank for just this occasion. It melted my heart! It made me see that Connie did not think that of me! She loved me even then and protected me! I needed to hear that little piece so much! Momma knew it too and when Bro. Rodney said that, she knew exactly how that would touch me and said, "See?" Like I said before, God orchestrates every item/every event of our lives. He had a young preacher catch a tiny, insignificant piece of two little girl's lives and store that in his memory bank to bless one of the sisters with on one of the hardest days of her life.

Connie & Cameron

Meanwhile back at my parent's house after the service:

Scriptures we were reminded of this night, but Scripture we should've been practicing with no reminder:

Luke 6:31-36 - " Here is a simple rule of thumb for behavior: Ask yourself what you want people to do for you; then grab the initiative and do it for them. If you only love the love-able, do you expect a pat on the back? Sinners do that. If you only help those who help you, do you expect a medal? Sinners do as much. ...I tell you, love your enemies. Help without expecting a return..." (MSG)

Romans 12:18 - "...be at peace with everyone" (KJV)

Later that night we were "touched by Connie". This was only the beginning, many more "episodes" followed. Many would say "Connie" isn't doing these things/that's not Biblical etc. We aren't claiming "she" is. We know God is allowing every bit of these things to happen. But no one knows what God allows those in heaven to participate in or suggest. We won't know that until we are there ourselves.

113

We were loading the car to go to Conway when someone pulled in. It was dark and we were lit by the garage but we couldn't see who was walking toward us. I will not name names for obvious reasons. When they got into view I was very surprised. Let me backup a bit: we, as a family dislike very few. In this case, this person hadn't wronged us directly. In this case, we knew something they had done and disliked based on that. Simply put, we played judge, which is wrong. This is not unlike what I mentioned earlier regarding my brother-in-law and the lady that took Connie's job. Normally, if this person had been in our presence we would avoid. Instead, tonight, I walked up to them and hugged them as did Momma. After they left, Momma and I were crying. We felt the same emotions: Connie

wanted us to begin life this point on growing in the Lord and letting go of any sin (judging, un-forgiveness being a start). We both felt so humbled and free if you will. We have no way of knowing if that person knew we had hard feelings toward them. Probably so because we made a point to avoid etc. We asked and still do, what brought that person by? They had never been to our home before, it wasn't like someone who visited or even had the opportunity to. No one else (other than Connie's best friend) came to Momma and Daddy's during this time, not a one! Yet, this one that we harbored ill feelings for came by. We weren't on their route either. They said they had driven by after work and felt led to come offer their condolences. We aren't on their route home- answer that. They were also the very first ones we received a memorial from. Their memorial arrived

114

almost freakishly fast. What a lesson of forgiveness and tolerance for us. I know I may be elaborating too much on this but it blows my mind. I can't think of one other soul we have hard feelings for and that is the ONE person that makes an appearance at our home! My friend commented how this ties in perfectly with when Connie approached the lady at the restaurant who took her job. A lesson of forgiveness.

I mentioned the party above giving a memorial. I'm going to take a moment to go into the past and connect to the memorials. When Connie first lost her job with Senior Care she, as I mentioned tried to work, moved several times and then ended up living with my parents. In total, I guess this process lasted a bit over 10 years. That's a long time to go without a steady income yet constantly be needing money. The moving costs, the new lodgings costs, the medical bills, medicines, basic needs... On and on. The debts mounted quickly. My parents faithfully took care of Connie for most of these years. I'm tempted to say the amount they spent but I'm not sure that's appropriate nor would they want me to. They never kept up with it. I did. I did because Connie had hoped one day to surprise them and pay them back. Suffice it to say, it was a great deal, enough to buy their home again nearly; yet they never kept a "tab", never expected or wanted it back, never "gave her a hard time" or made her feel bad for it. Frankly, they never brought it up.

1 Timothy 5:8 - "But if anyone does not provide for his relatives, especially for members of his household, he has denied the faith and is worse than an unbeliever." (ESV)

God used someone to help Connie in her desire to repay our parents. This was done because the Lord laid it on someone's heart. No one had or has any idea the need nor did they know of my parents' financial help to Connie. On the exterior, giving this help wasn't warranted. For personal reasons I can't get into that at this time, but suffice it to say, this help was a supernatural miracle, especially since the dire need was unknown.

Deuteronomy 15, Proverbs 19 abbr.- ... *"Lend to them (family) without expecting to get repaid...." ... "it is like lending to the Lord, the Lord will pay you back"* (ESV)

I realize I have and will possibly continue to overuse the words "supernatural"/"miraculous". First of all, can you misuse/overuse that if it is present? I heard someone say recently that in these last days if we are in tune with the Holy Spirit, if we seek His face in prayer, study His Word- our lives will be *"naturally supernatural"*.

I am about to get into the rest of the miracles we've witnessed. I want to be clear when I say we in no way feel "Connie" has the power to make all this happen. Absolutely not! No person alive or dead has power on their own. We do believe God uses His people, His angels in many ways. "Dead or alive" I've never taken thought of until now. I do have to add 2 Timothy 2:1 where it speaks of a being *"compassed about with so great a cloud of witnesses"*. Many commentaries and pastors teach that these witnesses are the saints who have gone on before us in addition to the angels.

 These recordings are not meant to be mind changing or belief altering. I am just reporting/testifying/recording what actually happened, not adding to or taking away. They are priceless to us, they are miraculous to us but, as we may discover *US* may be the operative word. That is ok if so, we will never downgrade or push aside what we've seen/heard. Let me also add that we all are a people of faith and integrity. I need to say this because for those that don't know us, you may think we are imagining or even worse making this up. Had I not seen most with my own eyes, I must confess much would be hard for me to accept. Imagine if Moses had to go home after walking across the Red Sea and explain that to his family and friends!

W-O-R-L-D: "I'll believe it when I see it."

W-O-R-D: "I believe what I can not see."

Hebrews 11:1 - "Now faith is the substance of things hoped for, the evidence of things not seen." (KJV)

Listen to the Living Bible translation of this: "What is faith? It is the confident assurance that something we want is going to happen. It is the certainty that what we hope for is <u>waiting</u> for us, even though we cannot see it up ahead."

Chapter 13
Guiding Hand

To us, "*Connie's Miracles*'" began in the hospital before she left

this earth, her appearance after, then her being late for the home-
going service and the service itself, and the rest. Had our "touches"
ended there, that would be enough to satisfy anyone but God wasn't
nearly finished as I'll do my best to describe.

We had Connie's burial in Hot Springs the day after the service. We
had almost reached Hot Springs when Burns asked if we could go to
the tower after the burial. Hot Springs has a observation tower that
he had gone to every time we went to Hot Springs to see Connie and
Don. My first "mother" reaction was a bit let down in him thinking
he'd even be thinking of going to that today of all days. Then I
thought, well, he just doesn't understand. I was afraid it would hurt
Momma and Daddy too that he would think of doing a tourist
attraction on today of all days. While I was thinking how I'd answer
him, Momma said, "Yes, you sure can...(something caught Momma's
eye and she shouted for us to "LOOK!")". What in the world was

she talking about?! Let me add, there wasn't one cloud in the sky! A beautiful solid blue sky EXCEPT for what Momma and Daddy saw. I missed it I'm sad to say because I was driving and they were talking with such excitement, we passed it before I understood what they were seeing.

Now to explain what Momma was so intent on us looking at:

You can see the tower from the highway. They said, after Burns asked that, a cloud in the form of a hand was pointing to that tower right above it!!!!!!! To be more specific, Momma said it was the exact shape of Connie's hand and arm!!!!! So you can understand now why I missed it; there was just a *tad* of excitement. I'm being facetious, they were so excited and talking so fast and furious it was hard to understand. So, needless to say we all went to the tower after the burial. Don even went with us (after hearing the story) and took Burns in. All that was <u>So Connie!</u> That is just what she would've wanted for Burns that day and yes that day of all days. I imagine if others had seen us doing that right after burying our daughter, wife, sister, aunt... they would've thought we were a bit "off".

We're not done yet, hang on! We went to the grave site before time to make sure we knew where it was, where she was etc. It was extremely windy that day. We pulled up to what we felt was the right place (my navigation messed up so we weren't even sure we were at

120

the right cemetery). Flowers/sprays were laid out, yet one small poinsettia at the edge of the road, closest to us tipped over. As if to say, "here I am Momma and Daddy, this is the right place". As I mentioned it was extremely windy. If anything should've tipped over, this short poinsettia would be the last. It was closest to the ground and was in a pot that had a wide enough bottom to keep it up. Yet it fell and those delicate tall sprays stayed upright. Momma was talking about that and then I turned my phone on to check for texts etc and I was shown a picture of Connie. You will say, "so?" This will be hard to convey without talking but I'll try. Remember I mentioned several pages back how Don took some pictures of Connie at the movie, "Christmas in Connecticut"? There was one in particular where she was in front of the movie's poster with her fist in the air (showing joy) and a HUGE smile. Honestly a bit too happy to just be at a movie. We see now, the Lord orchestrated that photo/that mood/that expression for this time, not that movie. Explanation: this picture had never been sent to my phone, viewed on my phone, or had any connection to my phone. The first time I saw this picture was the night before on my desktop. Since it had been taken such a short time before her illness, she had never sent to me. How did that picture get on my phone? How did it get on my wallpaper? AND, my phone is set up that each time I click it on, I see my wallpaper then I have to slide to unlock it. Not this time, I click the button and boom there's that picture full screen minus the clock, date, etc that is always on at the beginning, and I didn't even slide to unlock. So in sequence, this poinsettia falls and less than 10 seconds later I turn my phone on. So we "feel" (not saying we audibly heard her) her say, "Here I am..." then right after we see this joyful picture which makes us "feel" her saying: "Imagine where I am, what I'm seeing, who I'm seeing, what I'm doing...I'm WITH THE KING!!!!!"

As soon as I saw Bro. Rodney who was to perform the service I had to tell him all this. You can imagine how excited we were. He, a man of faith believed as well and even had me share during the service. Before the service, I couldn't find Burns. Momma and Daddy were waiting in the car along with Burns (I thought) since it was cold. I went to the car and Burns wasn't in there. Momma thought he had gotten out to be with me. Even though Burns is probably old enough to be on his own more, we still watch out for him super carefully. This was odd that Momma didn't watch him to make sure he did find me. She would never just let him out and "hope" he got to me. He's also super careful and cautious, so not the type to get out and start wondering around. Walking around and exploring, especially on his own is not his cup of tea. We began looking for him immediately. We were a bit concerned since it wasn't like him. I looked all around. Momma then saw him way off in the distance in the cemetery. He was looking at the headstones. As he walked back, Momma said he walked exactly like her daddy, my grandaddy. She had never seen that resemblance before. She carefully watched him the whole way and she was so taken by what she saw and felt such a peace as if her daddy was here today comforting her.

2 Thessalonians 3:16 - "Now the Lord of peace himself give you peace always by all means. The Lord be with you all." (KJV)

Shortly after, Mrs. Rickie (a special friend of Connie and Don) came up to Momma and Daddy. She is a special lady, Connie's first friend in Hot Springs. She's in her 80's and up until recently has enjoyed exceptional health. She loves a certain vitamin company and usually made sure Connie had some (no charge) and many times also gave them to my parents. Connie always tried to get them for Daddy especially. They were said to help with a condition Daddy has so Connie hoped one day to be able to afford to make sure Daddy always had. Mrs. Rickie told Momma to hold on, she went to her car and guess what she brought: those vitamins. She said oddly they were delivered to her just that morning. Odd? Nope. Connie wanted Daddy to have!

Matthew 7:11- "If ye then, being evil, know how to give good gifts unto your children, how much more shall your Father which is in heaven give good things to them that ask Him?" (KJV)

God shows us in so many ways daily (if we'll stop and ponder them all) how He cares for and about what we need, what we enjoy, what we want...

Before the service, Connie's best friend, Renee texted me. She had an odd thing happen. She had lost her husband 9 years ago this day. She went to her computer this morning and there was a old post from Connie. It was something Connie had written to encourage/console Renee after losing her husband. Renee couldn't explain how this showed up on her computer. Also, what was written was something that would console Renee this day for losing her dear friend.

Chapter 14
Jesus Take the Wheel, Faith Drives

After going to the tower, we all went to Don's parents'.

Momma was anxious, she was fidgety, wanting to leave seemed like. I didn't think that was bad or rude since she had been through so much. I just thought she was ready to be settled and be home versus being around others. I found out later that night that she had no idea why she felt like that, but it became clear the reason later. She did tell me when we got in the car that she had such an urgency to "go!". They had served food so we were really ok eating wise until the next day or until we got home. Yet, I suggested we go to an Italian restaurant that Burns and I had gone to once. I thought it was on the way home and not far. I used my GPS and it took us downtown. I had never driven down there before. Connie loved Hot Springs downtown during the Christmas season. She and Don had gone the Christmas before and she went on and on to Momma about it. Said it reminded her of an old 1940's movie. She mentioned to me as well that we should come up there. Oh how I wish we had, but I kept putting off thinking, yes, we will one of these days. So here we were right at dark seeing this beautiful scene Connie had described and loved so well. Me and Momma especially soaked this in and marveled at the fact the GPS had taken us this route where it had never before. Connie wanted her Momma to see that!

Well, here we go to the restaurant. Looking back, we can't understand other than God why in the world would we even be thinking of food. No one was hungry, everyone was ready to get home and get to bed. We were all exhausted emotionally and physically. Yet, here we head out to this restaurant that we had no idea really where it was, nor oddly enough, and hard to explain had no desire for. And normally, had we been thinking, if we had been hungry we would have just driven through the drive-through somewhere just to kill hunger and get on home. As we look back now, our thoughts were not directed by us at all, totally God was driving that car. Well, we drove and we drove and we drove. Mercy! I wish I knew how long. Burns was the first to let us know he was tired of driving as do all children and he pointed out that we must be going away from home because our mileage to home was increasing versus decreasing and by more than 50 miles!!!! What had I done, I thought. I was increasingly getting more and more exhausted then I began to get a bit confused at all this driving. It was like a dream sequence almost, just driving and driving in the dark and never reaching your destination. Finally we did. When I stepped out, my legs felt like noodles, I was at my limit! I was so tired! While we ate I began thinking how far we were from home! Fifty miles extra to drive on top of the long drive anyway. So, we had driven 50 miles extra both ways! If I could've laid on that floor at the restaurant and slept until morning I think I would have, my germaphobe self aside. I prayed as I ate that God would get us home safely and "quickly, Lord, quickly!" So, an hour almost later we are in Hot Springs AGAIN! It was as if we had been traveling on a hamster's wheel, spinning and spinning in a circle. I wanted to cry when I realized what I had done and the amount of driving still ahead of me. Oh me of little faith! God meant all this for our good as we later found. My GPS (in this part of the story aka the Holy Spirit) yet again took me a route I've never been. I was tired so basically just focusing on the road versus any scenery. Something (God) made me look to the left. It was Connie's hospital. I told everyone and we all noticed and marveled that it was GLOWING!! There was such a beautiful glow, a beautiful, glowing light completely covering it! And, on the roof we could see a cross! We didn't know if it was a transmitter or something just in the shape of a cross or an actual cross. Regardless, a cross was seen! Again, we aren't saying we heard Connie's voice but it gave us all the feeling of such peace and to me, Momma, and Daddy it said, "Look, everyone, this is where Jesus came for me!"

1 Corinthians 3:18 - "But we all, with unveiled face, beholding as in a mirror the glory of the Lord, are being transformed into the

127

same image from glory to glory, just as by the spirit of the Lord." (KJV)

Matthew 17:2 - "His face shone like the sun." (KJV)

[I'll add this now, we drove by the hospital December 2015 again, it was about the same weather, time of day etc and obviously same month. There was no glow. There was no cross that we could see.}

What I believe was on that hospital was the glow of the presence of the supernatural! Don't tell me this isn't Biblical or that I'm grasping. Someone from Glory came for Connie there. Was it Jesus himself, His angels, Grandmomma or Grandaddy? I don't know, but someone did, that IS Biblical.

Ministering Angels: Daniel 3: three men went in the fire, four came out!
1 Kings 19:5,6: an angel brought Elijah bread and water
Luke 16:22 - "The time came when the beggar died, angels carried him to Abraham's side." (KJV)

All Christians will see/experience this unless we go by way of the rapture and then we know who comes for us- Jesus will meet us in the clouds (1 Thessalonians. 4:17).

128

We continued home. We are still in Hot Springs when a car eases up alongside. Its dark, I'm tired as I can be, but that car interested me, grabbed my attention. Why? Tons of cars obviously had met us, passed us and none had interested me. We were on a four lane highway, I was in the far right lane. This car began to ease along side on my left. It was in the fast lane, yet seemed odd to me the speed it was traveling. It was passing ,but not like others pass; this I can't put into words, I'm sorry. I was fixed on that car. As it got closer I could see it was one of those cars that have an ad-wrap (I guess that's the term for cars completely covered in their business' logo etc). Since we seemed to be under this supernatural miraculous umbrella, we were super observant and aware of all of our surroundings. It was covered with this wrap, but I couldn't tell what the business was. I saw a elderly person pictured and then got even more curious. The car eased along side, again not gaining much speed; it was as if we were both in slow motion. I told Momma to start looking as well now. I'm not sure who noticed first because it seemed we yelled it out simultaneously. On the rear of the car written the length of the car was...

"SENIOR CARE"!! Remember that name? (where Connie worked as the director; in case I failed to mention earlier- Connie was the one who named the unit "Senior Care") You talk about chill bumps and tears!!!!!! We have never, ever seen a car with this logo, a billboard, an ad, you name it- we've never seen that company name anywhere other than when Connie worked there. What in the world was going on we thought? We followed that car for the next 30-45 minutes. They never got out of our sight. It was when we got to I430 (almost to Little Rock) that Momma suggested getting along side to see "who" could be driving. Boy, let me tell you, at this point we were on a <u>miracle high</u> if I can use that term. We were pumped up and praising the Lord. First I pulled alongside to see what I could see. What I saw almost made me wreck. **I saw Grandmomma!** I didn't dare say out loud what I saw. What if I'm seeing things, that would hurt Momma, Momma has been through enough today... I kept quiet although I was about to explode. Momma said she couldn't see the driver and asked me to change lanes so the car would be on her side. Fearfully, I must admit, I did. She <u>screamed,</u> "Momma! Its Momma! Cameron, its Momma!" Over and over while crying she kept shouting that, just that. What else could she say? I just cried along with her saying, "Yes, I know, Momma, I see her too!" The driver (I hate to say that, I want to say "Grandmomma" because that is "who" this "driver" was!) stared straight ahead. We had to be conspicuous the way we kept going from lane to lane and getting right alongside. Any driver would look to see who was along side, that's just common reaction from any driver. She never moved, she

130

kept her hands in the same position and never moved! It was late so
there wasn't much traffic and here we were hovering, if you will over
this car; going back and forth switching from lane to lane so the
other could see and she never turned her head!   It was time for us to
exit onto I630. "Grandmomma" wasn't exiting, it was clear, so before
I got onto the ramp I said, "Goodnight, Grandmomma!" At that
moment, she put her right turn signal on as if to respond. She had
not used that signal before now even as she changed lanes; believe
me we would have noticed; we were glued to that car. She had no
reason to use her signal at this moment.   She wasn't turning, she was
going straight down the road. It was her right signal; I was going
right. The road was bending just a bit to the left so if she even
needed her turn signal at this point it would have been left not right!
Even the signal itself was off/odd. We've studied turn signals since
and have never seen one like that. Most car's turn signals are on top
or connected to the brake light and are smaller. This was a huge
rectangle, super visible. We guessed it to be about a 9x7 inch
rectangle. That's huge. The light color was off/odd too. We've
studied that since too and can't duplicate. It was the brightest,
strangest yellow. Not the strangest yellow though as I'm about to
explain. I have shared this story with very few. One friend
questioned why we didn't keep following her. She said, "I would've
followed mine had I seen her to the ends of the earth!" That's
exactly what I would say to anyone too that told me this story. God
was directing us, that's all I can say. It wasn't His will for us to follow

her on, force her off the road (yes, I even now wonder why we didn't do that!), try to get her attention etc.

We continued toward home. We are now on the ramp leading to I40. This will be very hard to put into words as well. As we round the corner we see...boy this is hard to explain in words! We see a light like we've never seen on this earth, not unlike that turn signal, but its covering the entire left side of the grassy area next to our ramp. Its a light that's so bright it hurts your eyes, yet its peaceful at the same time. Amongst the light were a lot of people (I'd guess at least 50) construction workers we thought then because what else could they be?! Momma and I commented just a bit on that, but not long. We were confused literally. We spoke and do speak now a lot about it, recalling what we saw but we didn't comment much then. You know it doesn't take long to take a ramp onto the interstate but it seemed we were going in slow motion. Those "workers" were like dark shadows. Whenever you see construction workers on the interstate, day or night you can always tell even if far away what they are wearing: jeans, hats or no, you can see the beards on the men or not, boots or tennis shoes, etc. My point is, you can always tell/see the people even when you're going full speed. You probably couldn't recognize them if you saw later face to face but you get my point, you can see them. We couldn't see these people. They were just dark shadows; albeit absolutely nothing frightening or disturbing. I have to add this now, believe me if I was reading this or hearing this from someone I would have a hard time accepting. It's hard for me even to recall and rationalize it. I've often tried since to visualize it enough to draw it but I can't, not sure I could if I were an artist. We've come to the conclusion that we can't rationalize it; it was just miraculous. That was our (everyone's in the car) recollection of the drive home until we got onto the last road in Conway to our house. None of us remember anything (talking, the drive, etc) from seeing that scene until that Conway road (that is about 30 minutes). When we exited I40 onto the Old Morrilton Hwy, Daddy spoke first and said, "How'd we get here so fast?" I was driving of course, but I felt like I woke up from a dream when I heard his voice. Then all began chiming in the same, "How <u>did</u> we get here so fast!". Everyone in the car had the same experience, the same loss of time, the same feeling they'd just woken from a dream (a dream with no memory). It's odd to us that Daddy was the first to ask this. He never pays any attention while he's traveling to even notice where we are, if we arrived late or early. I'll ask it because I know you must be thinking it: were we transported? what happened? I do not know! So I will not humanize it or try to add to make it make sense in the natural. I just trust that the Lord gave us a special, extra special divine encounter that entire day and I'm thankful for it regardless if I can explain or understand it. Why us? I don't know that either. God doesn't always have to spell things out for us. We just have to "trust and obey for there's no other way".

Matthew 19:26 - " Jesus looked at them and said, With man this is impossible, but with God all things are possible." (NIV)

I guess you must think this is the end of *Connie's Miracles*, right?

For us, it sure could've been. How miraculous the sights we've seen, but God wasn't finished and I don't think is finished. I began writing this several years ago now (and counting) and I've added things continually in my notebook since. I wonder if these things will go on until we leave this earth; that would be ok with us for sure.

Not too many days after losing Connie, Don brought Connie's car ("the Juke") by so Burns could see one last time. Burns was driving it up and down the driveway. The key fell off the dash into the floor. When I was trying to find it, I saw something between the seats. It was the receipt from Hobby Lobby, the one that had her wreath on it. The other was a brochure from where she'd gotten her nails done on December 5, just one week before she passed away. She and Don had gone to a reunion on the 6th. She told momma how excited she was to get her nails done. Said she hadn't gotten them done since their wedding. She had occasions like the reunion to get them done before and didn't. She just *thought* she was getting them done for that reunion! She had a much greater appointment than that coming! Also laying in the same spot as the receipt and brochure was the menu from the restaurant she and a friend had gone to that last time in Wynne. Don had already cleaned the car and he apparently hadn't seen these. There were no gum wrappers, straw paper, coins- just these 3 papers. I kept them and am looking at now even. They meant something to Connie and were meant to be saved in that car. In the glove box was the CD (Ivan Parker) that Connie had bought for the Terry's. Of all the discs she could've bought that day, this one was made in 1998. 1998 was the year that Connie's life changed. That was the year that began her struggle physically, yet was what molded her to the woman she became.

"Grief is like a long valley, a winding valley where any bend may reveal a totally new landscape." C. S. Lewis

Chapter 15
Miracles Continue

Luke 1:37 - "For with God nothing shall be impossible." (KJV)

Deuteronomy 10:21 - "He is the one you praise; He is your God, who performed for you those great and awesome wonders you saw with your own eyes." (KJV)

Daddy's birthday is December 17. We weren't sure if we would

even mention it this year, just 5 days after Connie's passing. But Connie had other ideas. Connie was habitually late as I've said many times. This year though for Christmas and Daddy's birthday, she'd shopped early. Odd? Nope, God knew and he nudged her to get ready, be ready. She had ordered Daddy's present and knew it was to be delivered soon. The Tuesday before Connie passed away she had Don (she didn't feel like talking) call Momma to tell her to be watching for it; it arrived that day. Momma saved it and told Daddy to wait and open when Connie came. Of course, that never happened. So, on Daddy's birthday, Momma gave him Connie's gift. Daddy's gift was a Tervis cup with a *St. Louis Cardinals* insignia. That is Daddy's favorite team. What's odd is that even though Daddy likes them, we aren't ones to buy things with logos on like that. It would have been more Connie's style to have his name on or something. We discovered later why the "cardinal"!

That was the first holiday/event to be taken care of miraculously. I'll add now, more than two years after her passing, not a birthday, anniversary, gift giving holiday has passed without a "touch" from Connie!

This first Christmas like I mentioned was a numb time for all of us. So thankful that God nudged Connie to prepare early. She had Burns' gift and even the next Christmas as I found out later. We all had a gift from Connie that year. *My gift* was a bit strange. Not a strange item, strange circumstances. Connie had lost quite a bit of weight in the last year or so. She and I had never really had the same taste in clothes, not worlds apart but different nonetheless. When she started losing she began buying new clothes (she was NO stranger to buying things).

After she had bought a few things, Momma said, "these look like Cameron". She told me later, "I want to start dressing like you". When she told me, she had that Connie smirk that could mean several things. It could mean: I'm being sneaky or even: I want to cry but don't want to so I'll use this expression to show my love. The latter will only make sense to me and maybe 3 others.

She'd ordered a winter coat. It came right before Thanksgiving. She'd tried it on but never wore, the tags were still on it. Don brought it to me. It was my size, it was exactly what I would've chosen! I loved it! It so wasn't what she normally picked for herself.

Thank you, Lord and "thank you, sweet sister!"

On January 2, 2015 I was at my parents' home. Momma and I were looking in Connie's room (she had lived there for 8 years before marrying Don). Momma pulled out a white box. She was about to ask me if I wanted it when I asked her what it was; I couldn't remember it. I had seen it, of course, always out on Connie's dresser etc but I couldn't remember what it was. Before she opened it, she told me the story. So glad she told me before opening.

It was called a *Worry Box*. When Connie was a counselor on the drug and alcohol unit, a patient gave to her. Momma said there was a poem on the inside and crystal angels. The poem read: "This is your worry box. The angels within your heart, a place to tuck away fears, where love and prayer can start. So keep this box beside you and know how much God cares. For when you need peace and joy, the angels will be there." After hearing the story, momma opens the box.

Her reaction was, well she was speechless except to just hand it to me- All the angels were crushed! I wish this was a video versus a written account. I've tried telling this story to others and without actually showing them the box, it's almost impossible to explain. I'll try. The box itself is a tapestry box, delicate. The lid closes but doesn't lock or fasten in any way; it just lays closed. The angels are nestled very snug in a formed styrofoam bed then has cotton surrounding each form. The form of the styrofoam is deep, the angels more than halfway down in that "hole" and its super tight. Each angel was still snug in its base (styrofoam), yet the wings were broken off of each and much of their bodies were shattered. The upper bodies and wings were loose in the box. Some pieces were large breaks and some super tiny shards of glass. This is impossible. We have played out every scenario to make it possible and can't. Just to pretend: if someone threw it down on concrete, the box would be dented (it's very delicate) and the pieces that broke would be scattered all over the floor and the angel's bodies wouldn't be in place. Regardless of playing out certain scenarios, the only ones who would've had in their possession to break would be Connie, Momma, or me. None of us ever dropped. Also, this has always been in a room with carpet. Had someone even chunked it to the floor with force, carpet wouldn't shatter the glass like this. Had it shattered, the tiny pieces or even large broken pieces would be on floor not in the box. Plus, if any one of us had broken, we would have thrown away. To us, its clear.

Momma and I were both reminded of what Bro. Jolly said at Connie's funeral: "Connie has lost her faith...she no longer needs it!". Re read what the worry box poem said. Connie doesn't need any of that described! Did God shatter those right when Connie was taken? We firmly believe, YES.

1 Corinthians 15:54-57 - "Then, when our dying bodies have been transformed into bodies that will never die, the Scripture will be fulfilled: Death is swallowed up in victory. O death, where is your victory? O death, where is your sting? For sin is the sting that results in death, and the law gives sin its power. But thank God! He gives us victory over sin and death through Jesus." (NLT)

Philippians 3:20,21 - "But our homeland is in heaven, where our Savior is; and we are looking forward to his return from there." (TLB)

This world is not my home, I'm just passing through!

140

A few days later I headed back to Conway, I was overcome with grief. I was crying so hard I thought I'd have to pull over because I couldn't see. At that moment, I saw a covey of red birds (cardinals) feeding on the side of the road. I'm not up on my bird facts, but regardless it touched me. I didn't understand why, but I stopped crying and had a funny recollection of Connie. On the way home I kept thinking, wonder if there is something to seeing a grouping of cardinals like that or even seeing "cardinals". When I got home I checked my Facebook for messages regarding Connie. When I pulled it up there was a story about cardinals right there, the very first post! The post hadn't tagged me nor was it sent to me. It was a post showing a grouping of cardinals and explaining that many feel when they see them, especially a group (found out from Daddy who knows birds that cardinals don't gather in large groups like that as a norm) that its God's way of comforting us when we are sad for losing someone. Wow! I couldn't believe this newsfeed was on at this moment. I didn't scroll down past others posts, it was first! Imagine that post being there for me to see at that time! This began the cardinal story. Every day since, Momma and Daddy have always had at least one cardinal sighting. They have bird feeders, yet never in all the years living in Wynne has even one cardinal come to their home.

This same event happened once more when I returned to Wynne the next time. Again, it was a grouping of them right when I was very upset. And again I stopped crying and felt like smiling. On June 17, 2015, Momma noticed there hadn't been any cardinals that day. At that moment she heard in her head, "just a minute, Momma" and

then there were two! Also, on 6/12/15 (6 month anniversary of
Connie's leaving) when Momma woke, she saw two on her window
sill. Again, to this day, years passing and there has not been a day
that Momma doesn't see cardinals in the yard. Again on August 2,
2016 momma realized she hadn't seen one and said, "Connie, I
haven't seen one today." Within seconds there two appeared.
Sometime in mid January 2015, I was in Wynne again. We were
looking in Connie's closet. We found one book. Connie loved to
read and loved to collect books almost as much. She had them
displayed on shelves in Momma's living room. So, why this one
lonesome book in here by itself? We had to investigate since we've
been shown so many things. The book itself didn't hold a meaning
for us so we opened. Inside there was something written inside from
one of Connie's friends. The note didn't hold anything for us either.
I thought the note was written directly on the page until I looked
closer then saw it was a card. It was deceiving because the card was
blank except for the note and the card stock was the same color as
the page. Plus it was almost stuck to the pages so it looked flush. I
closed the card and guess what was on the cover: a huge red cardinal!
No wording, just that cardinal! There has continued to be
connections with cardinals.
Around the middle of January 2015, an odd thing happened and again
shortly after. Burns was sleeping in my bed. I turned to look at him
and at the same time my body felt so strange- it was as if my heart
wasn't beating- he WAS Connie. Many say he favors Connie even
more than me. I'm not talking about favoring at this point. His face

was her's! And oddly it wasn't at any age I've ever seen her. She wasn't young or her present age. I can't explain it any better than that. Burns could tell something had bothered me and asked me. Just a couple minutes later it happened again.

On May 23, 2015 it happened again. This time he was getting a hair cut. I wasn't thinking of her per say, I wasn't staring at him to try and get my mind to see her. It just happened, on each of the occasions. Speaking of "seeing" Connie, in February 2015, we were driving and Burns gasped. He does this often when he sees a "cool car". He loooooooves cars so I hear this gasp quite often. I didn't ask him right away which car he'd seen. I guess I was thinking of something else. He usually waits until I ask and if not he's ok with not even sharing what he saw. This time he said, "Momma! I just saw a Juke (Connie's car). I just saw Aunt Connie! She was driving it!" I'm going to end there and not even explain. I think so many things have been explained that by now you understand that miracles just can't be explained. I will say this: Burns is literal, beyond literal at times. He doesn't try to "see" things. I could explain Burns more, but trust me when I say I didn't hesitate to believe him. I did ask just to satisfy myself was it someone who just looked a lot like her. I should've trusted him, he shot that down right away and said, "it was Aunt Connie; I saw HER, Momma!"

April 4, 2015 was the day before Easter. Connie always got Burns a card and present on Easter and was usually here if she could. That day/night I was sad thinking Burns wouldn't hear from her this year. When will I learn not to be sad first, but to trust! I'm not sure which way to tell this story. I think I'll tell it as it happened and explain it in the order I found out. On Easter Sunday, Burns hunted his eggs before church like always (inside). We pulled out of the garage to head to church when I saw a strange site. Our side flower bed had purple (I will explain the "purple" meaning later) eggs! What in the world?! Who had done this and in the night? Burns was already watching his DVD so he hadn't seen, I had to show him. He didn't doubt, he didn't wonder; he said, "AUNT CONNIE!!!!!" Oh ye (me) of little faith thought, well, bless his heart I'll let him think that. He gathered them and each was filled with a different increment of cash. The total was $100! I then thought, bet it was my friend who lives down the street. When we got home I called her to thank her, thinking it was her. It was her alright, but not her idea! She's super thoughtful and this sounds like something she would've planned for weeks ahead knowing Connie's story and knowing Burns would think it was from Connie. My friend is so thoughtful and always does things way ahead of time so this sounded right up her alley. Not the case! She said she wished she had thought of it, but she couldn't take the credit. I thought, what?

This is what she told me: she had already gone to bed and taken care of her children's baskets. It was about midnight and she just couldn't fall asleep. Something kept gnawing at her. She couldn't get settled. Then she said all this just came to her. She said it wasn't like her thoughts, hard for her to put into words she said. She was told in her head to get purple eggs and put $100 in and lay them out for Burns! She then said to herself: What? Purple? $100? She told me she'd already done the eggs for her children and had no idea if she had any eggs left much less purple! And $100? She said she rarely if ever has cash in her wallet. She got up though and checked. She had $100 exactly! She had purple eggs! Get this, she had just enough purple eggs to account for the $100! She had 1's, 5's...and change that totaled $100 <u>exactly</u> and had the <u>exact</u> number of eggs to accommodate that amount! She woke her husband and out they went in the night to hide them! She admitted she knew exactly who had told her to do that! She joked (knowing Connie always waited till the last minute and was a night owl) and said next time she hoped Connie would let her know a bit earlier! The $100 amount kept gnawing at me and then it hit me! Connie had wanted to get Burns a kitten for Christmas. She had asked me, but I said we really needed to wait until we moved. She had planned on writing Burns a check and give it to him Christmas (2014) to save for whenever we could get his kitten; her plan was to give $100!!!!!! Mercy! So, Burns has "Aunt Connie's $100" in his account waiting for when we can get his kitten **from Aunt Connie!**

December 2016, we did get Burns' cat. Although this part isn't connected per say with this story, I as a mother have to add it to brag on Burns a second. Due to our financial and lodging situation, it just hadn't been the right time to

145

get a pet. In October 2016 I decided it was time regardless. Realized
I better start acting out what I preach about faith and step out in it,
timing "humanly" right or no.   I assumed Burns would head to the
car that moment. I was wrong, instead he said, "no, its not time yet;
God will tell me when." I said I wouldn't mention again then, I'd let
him tell me. It wasn't until December 19 that he said it was time and
said God told him to go on the 21st. So, on the 21st we went and the
perfect cat was there for him. She wasn't a kitten like we'd planned,
but Burns said one look at her and he knew kitten or no, she was the
one. This one part though does tie in with the story I felt- Let me
start by saying, she (aka "Feez") is extremely well behaved. Since her
arrival, she hasn't knocked anything over nor gotten on anything she
shouldn't (which is strange because we've not scolded her not to). My
point in saying that is one night about 4 weeks ago, I came in and got
this "manuscript" to work on. I've been working on it off and on
since Connie left. I came to a block I guess you'd say and put it away
for several months. This night I felt led to get it back out and work
on it, to finish it I'd hoped. I had just gotten it and returned to my
room when I heard something fall. Feez had gotten in an area she
had never and of all things here, knocked over Connie's picture. I
didn't see her do it, only after. I can't see based on where this picture
frame was, how in the world she even got to it much less knock it out
of the shelf. I smiled and said, "ok, Connie, I'll get on it (the book)".
The picture was unharmed and face up. Feez hasn't since been on
that built-in or anything else to be mischievous much less knock
anything over. Another odd thing to us is when we got Feez, the lady

146

at the store said, "This is strange, we don't have any information on her." She began looking all through the notes and couldn't find any information on her history. She said, "I'm sorry I can't provide you with anything other than her checkup records we did; this is very strange, we always have their history, at least a little." Hmmm...

God cares about the small things as well as the large. In this case, a little boy's promised kitten...

Luke 12:7 - "But even the very hairs on your head are all numbered..." (KJV)

Matthew 6:8 - " ...your Father knoweth what things ye have need of, before ye ask Him." (KJV)

March 28 is Connie and Don's wedding anniversary. We had wondered what might take place today. Connie loved snow as I mentioned. It was late in the year of course for Arkansas for snow. Momma called me though and said it was snowing in Wynne! Snowing?! It wasn't even cold enough for snow! Momma cried so saying Connie had asked the Lord to send it! To my knowledge, it didn't snow any other place in Arkansas that day. Connie didn't forget Don on this day either though. He had taken his boys hiking (see, it was hiking temp elsewhere, NOT SNOW!) to one of he and Connie's favorite spots. Get this for timing: on the very spot that Connie had wanted to have their wedding, a wedding was going on! Someone was getting married on their spot at the very time Don was hiking! Boy!!! Weddings don't last all day, there was probably a 30 minute window here. Don could've hiked at any time. The wedding could've been over by the time he got there or not even started. I think you get the idea! A blessing to Momma that spoke to her and a blessing to Don that spoke to him both connecting them to Connie on this special day.

John 14:27 - "Peace I leave with you, my peace I give unto you; not as the world giveth, give I unto you. Let not your heart be troubled, neither let it be afraid." (KJV)

Momma & Daddy

April 9, 2015 was Momma and Daddy's 50th wedding anniversary.
Such a milestone at such a hard time. Connie had asked me as early
as their last anniversary what I thought we should do for them. She
wanted so badly to make that day special. So hard to know that and
not have her there. Momma wanted this day to be very low key. She
didn't want much said about it, too hard without Connie. Burns and
I went to Wynne and we all went to Memphis for the day. We had
lunch at the Elegant Farmer. We had never been, I had seen on a
show on Food Network so we tried it. I wondered if Connie would
play a part in this day.

The owner had come by earlier to greet us as he did all the tables. He
had on a button down shirt (I have a reason for mentioning this).
Nothing odd so far. The meal was great, but nothing connected with
Connie. That's ok though, she's late remember so I hadn't given up.

149

It was dessert time now. Momma and Daddy ordered coconut cake. Momma teared up when she took her first bite. She said, "This is exactly like Momma's! I've never had one since that tasted like hers!" Grandmomma was an excellent cook, one of those that didn't need a recipe. I faintly remember her coconut cake and I haven't had one like it since either. I tried and sure enough, I was taken back to a little girl in Caldwell. We were satisfied with the Lord giving us that sweet touch. During that, the owner came back by (why we don't know because he seemed busy and had already greeted us; he didn't seem like the chatty type). I was so busy eating my cake I didn't hardly look up. Burns pulled on me and said, "Look what he's wearing, Momma!" He had changed shirts (why???) and now had on a **purple "Life Is Good" shirt!** I didn't explain that earlier so I will now. Connie's color was purple and her brand was "Life is Good". She really liked that brand and had a lot of and had dressed Don in it as well. I wasn't a fan of it, but she loved it. I can't say I have a "brand". And I can't say I have a color. She did and her closest friends knew it. Boy, God is good and so sweet to touch us like this! What a kind and gentle God we serve who cares about all the details of our lives and knows what speaks to our hearts! Precious!

On April 20, 2015, Renee, Connie's closest friend was having a hard day. She and Connie were extremely close and had been since they were little. Renee has grieved so much over Connie. Renee knows loss all too well. She lost her sister to cancer, her husband to the same, and both her parents. Connie's loss has hit her as hard as that of a sister. There have been things shown to Renee as well. I plan to get with her one day and record them. She has shared some with me already. On this day in particular, she was missing Connie a lot. She went to a drawer to get something and she found a card Connie had sent her. It was sent during the time she lost her husband and was meant as a consolation for him. She was also telling Renee how much she meant to her etc. In other words, it was a card that could've been sent in the present and fit Renee's present grief. Renee told me she keeps Connie's cards together elsewhere. She couldn't explain why this card was misplaced and here today. Thank you, Lord for ministering to us all!

April 26 is Burns' Jesus birthday (the day he got saved). We celebrate that each year as much as his physical birthday. Connie never forgot any date attached to Burns. I'm a bit forgetful with dates, but Connie never had to be reminded. She even kept up with our cat's (Uncle Felix) birthday. Uncle Felix passed away four years ago and she still continued to call me on his birthday.

I was a little sad this birthday (Burns' Jesus birthday), it would be the first without a card, present, or phone call to Burns from his Aunt Connie. Not to worry though! She had him a present...

Connie had a storage unit in Wynne. When she moved in with my parents she had to store many of her things. When she and Don married, they had planned to live in his home for a short time and then buy a home of their own. She wanted to wait until then to move her things. We had intended emptying that for weeks, months but Momma just wasn't ready. Something prompted her though to go there 3 days prior to Burns' birthday. She wasn't planning on emptying of course, just wanted to take a look at what was there. There were oodles of boxes. She decided to open one to see what was inside. She picked one at random that was labeled bedding/towels. It was towels, yet on the top was a box, a game turns out. It was called "Mancala". She took it home and called me. She had no idea what this was or why was a single game put in a box with towels. She had never seen this game before and turns out I hadn't either. So? you say- Connie moved several times as I mentioned early on in the story. Each time she moved Momma and I were the packers and unpackers. So, had this or anything been packed, we would have packed it. Neither of us had ever seen this game. And we surely wouldn't have packed a single game with a bunch of towels. We also knew everything Connie owned. We knew because we packed her each time plus we just knew what each of us had. We are a close family and we know what each other has etc. Momma knew right away this was meant for Burns' birthday. So she brought it to him. I can't remember if Momma discovered this or Burns- Guess the brand of this game: "CARDINAL"! and there is a single red cardinal by the brand. Mercy! Momma knew it was meant for Burns obviously, but was thinking he would just keep as a remembrance. Burns isn't a fan much of board games. Nope, he loves it! We play it several times a week and he even takes when we go to Wynne. You did good, Connie! You knew that though didn't you? Think of the timing of this even. Momma hadn't gone to that storage, but yet felt led three days prior to Burns' birthday! Hmm... God is so good!

The next holiday coming up was Mother's Day. I thought, ok, Connie covered Christmas, Daddy's birthday, her wedding anniversary, Momma and Daddy's anniversary, Easter, and Burns' Jesus birthday–would she cover Mother's Day? Momma had said she needed some new shoes. Said she really needed a black casual pair and a dress shoe. The Saturday before Mother's Day, Don came. He told Momma he'd brought her some <u>shoes</u> of Connie's! Don had no idea momma mentioned just before needing some shoes!!!!! She'd only mentioned casually to me. Momma and Connie wore the same size, but Connie had many styles that Momma couldn't wear or didn't such as boots etc. He brought several, but guess what fit: black casual and dress!!! Plus a bonus: a casual **purple** pair! That one is Momma's favorite obviously. The purple pair we didn't recognize and they looked brand new so we figured Connie bought late last summer to wear this season.

Before Don arrived, Momma was cleaning out a dresser. She pulled out a book and of all things it was a devotional book Connie had given her years ago.

When did she give it? Mothers's Day! How did we remember?
Connie had written a note to Momma in the book! Why did she
clean this out today? Why was this the book pulled out? We know
why!

May 12, 2002
Mother's Day

Momma,
    I would have never
found God, peace & hapiness
without the lifelong example
you & daddy have shown
me, both in words, but
even more so in your actions.
I hope this little book
blesses you as it has me.
No other mother deserves it
more.
            Love,
                Con

One day mid May, after we had cleared out Connie's storage unit, we were going through all the things. We were deciding what to keep, who to keep, and what to sell. Momma pulled out a platter and said how much she'd always liked it. I said, "well then you for sure keep that." She began tearing up a bit and said, "No, Renee will have this". I asked her why since obviously she liked it so. She said, "I have no idea why I remember this but Bobbie Lewis (one of Renee's aunts that passed away several years ago, a beloved aunt) gave this to Connie. That was in 1991 at Connie's first wedding shower. How in the world Momma recalled that?! I asked if she remembered who gave anything else and she laughed a bit and said, "I don't think I do." On the back of the platter was a sticker (odd because Momma is funny about stickers and always takes them off then washes the item even if its a decor piece) that said, "Morris Antiques Hot Springs". Hot Springs! Nothing else in all the belongings had a sticker left, nothing!

Chapter 16
Joy comes in the 'Mourning'

Christmas 2015 was to be our 2nd one without her. That first

Christmas (2014) was so close in time to her passing that we were all numb I think. Had it not been for Burns, I imagine we would've chosen to let it go by quietly. I recall that first Christmas (2014) Don asking me about a pen he'd found. Like I mentioned earlier, Connie had shopped uncharacteristically early that year. He asked me if I had any idea who she could've bought it for or maybe she'd told me. I didn't know. I had meant to have him bring to me, but with everything else going on, it slipped my mind. He tucked it away and now I'm so glad he did. He brought it back up this Christmas (2015). I still didn't know for whom she had bought it, but said maybe if I saw it I would be better able to guess. He brought it and one look I knew! It was for Burns no doubt. Don didn't need convincing after my reaction. I took one look at it and began weeping. Burn's daddy collected pens. I could see clearly in Connie's thoughtful head. This was a version for Burns not exactly like his daddy's which again she knew Burns wouldn't want. It looked just like "Burns", yet was such a precious connection to his daddy. I couldn't have picked a better one myself. So thankful Burns had a gift from Aunt Connie this Christmas too. So meant to be that Don saved it. There is more to the significance to this pen, but I'm not ready to explain that. It caused me to weep for many reasons. Reasons I felt Connie knew at the time when in fact humanly there is no way she could've. This in time will be so meaningful (even more than now) to Burns and to me now. Supernaturally God gave her this knowledge and knew the pen would be needed. Why so much emphasis on just a pen? Without the whole story I can see why you'd ask that. The season I'm going through now is a hard one. Hard in more ways than one. A season in which I desperately have needed Connie, her advice, her interest, her ability to reason things out... Getting this pen for Burns had advice, interest, and reason all wrapped up in a simple pen. This may only make sense to me, probably so. "Thank you, sweet sister!"

June 21, 2015 was Father's Day. We didn't go to church that day. Going to Caldwell Baptist (our home church and where the funeral was) on a regular Sunday is hard but on special occasions it's too hard. Burns and I drove up and took Momma and Daddy to lunch in Jonesboro. They usually have a huge crowd/wait at this place on Sundays especially. Today, they weren't busy at all and no wait, no one was waiting, immediate seating. We placed our drink orders and guess time got away and then Momma realized how long we'd waited

157

to get our drinks. The rest of the meal wasn't any better as far as timing. Late, late, late! The wait for everything we needed was almost comical.

Various waiters even came to our table to help our waitress. All around us people were being served normally (we watched) and even our waitress' other tables. We couldn't figure it out and almost got tickled at the

"When God decides to bless you, He will cause situations to come together in your favor…no matter what others try to do."- Christie Joyner

God has a purpose behind every problem.

When you put God first you will never be last.

craziness of the situation. Momma asked our waitress more than once what was going on and why just us. The answers made no sense. The manager came and his answer was just a silly. We just listened. We weren't upset acting or anything, just asking. He said, "Lunch is on me today, and please each one of you get a dessert too." (frankly, he seemed bewildered too) Well, we've had issues at restaurants before as has everyone, but we've never been given the whole meal free (for just timing issues) and desserts offered on top of that. Then the waitress came and handed us, from the manager, 2 $20 gift cards in addition. Momma said, "Connie! Carlton, Connie paid for your Father's Day lunch!" She said, "Yesterday I thought, wonder if Connie will do anything for Carlton tomorrow?"

So far, there have been more holidays, all of which we have been given a touch about Connie. Some are hard to convey in words, you would've had to been there to understand. They surely blessed us. December 12, 2015 was the first anniversary of Connie's passing. We went to Branson. We ate lunch at Mel's Diner. I went to pay and the cashier said, its been paid. By who? I have no idea. We don't know a soul in Branson. The waiter hadn't, we had no negative issues with the meal to warrant it etc. Who? I said, well, I will at least leave the tip. He said, "no ma'am that was paid too". I just stood there and cried right in that man's face. He probably thought boy she sure does appreciate this and he was right, but I was crying for another reason more so, connecting this blessing to this date. Thank you, Lord!

Psalm 23:4 - "Even though I walk through the darkest valley, I will fear no evil, for you are with me; your rod and your staff,
they COMFORT *me."* (ESV)

Then we walk out and right in our face was a dog identical to the one Connie had. (Clairie was her name, another of Connie's "children"; Connie had lost her several years ago). That made us smile. Meanwhile Don was back in Hot Springs. He and Connie didn't eat out a lot. There was however a restaurant they'd been to a bit, one of their favorites. They had sat in a particular booth. Today, Don wanted to eat here for Connie. He and his parents went and without asking for it or even thinking of it, the waitress sat him in that very booth. Earth shattering? No, but did it mean the world to him? Yes.

Mother's Day 2016 we were eating lunch here in Conway. We were waiting in the lobby for a table. We were standing in almost a circle formation: me, Momma, Daddy, and Burns. I was thinking in my head observing the circle we had formed and I noticed it wasn't closed, there was a space enough for one more. I smiled a bit thinking to myself, that's Connie's place. That alone made me smile then it happened- I smelled her! I haven't mentioned that yet in the story, let me explain.

Beginning here, I may skip around a bit time wise. Connie had a smell (before you react, it was a good smell). Not her perfume, not her laundry detergent, just her. I'd commented on that for years saying "I don't think I have a 'smell'". Then we'd laugh. Strange that she did. I use essential oils etc in my laundry and such and yet you know the smells never last. I'm sure tons of people use fragrances in their laundry only to find after one day in the drawer it's gone. Not Connie's. Strangely her clothes still smell like her, the scent hasn't gone. That's not possible. Something even stranger is Don's clothes don't have that smell and why not, she washed his the same as hers, he washes now like she did. Don gave me some of Connie's clothes. I've worn them a lot, washed many times and still that smell! Explain that!

[I'll interject this although over a year later than this Mother's Day event, here I sit today, almost three years after her passing, wearing

160

her shirt and the smell is overwhelming! When I put it on, I asked Burns to sniff and he said, "yep, still as potent as ever." What a blessing to sit here writing about her, thinking of her and still being able to smell her as if she was sitting right here.]

We're approaching the three year anniversary of Connie's passing. For reasons that are puzzling to us, these smells are escalating and becoming odder and odder. Recently Burns and I went to church at Caldwell with my parents. I wore a fur vest of mine. I had gotten it out of the cleaner's bag just that morning. It had been there since last winter. I wore it all day. I took it off on the ride home. I put back on and the smell was so strong of Connie and it had no smell prior! This is the first time clothing that wasn't hers has smelled. The next time was just two days later. Burns came in with his laundry basket full of clean towels. He said, "put your nose in here!" Yes, all the towels smelled. Later in the week, Don brought some of Connie's clothes, shoes, and Christmas tree. When you open those boxes it is so strong. How in the world can shoes and a Christmas tree smell like someone and three years after?! Days after that, Momma bought a sweater. When she got home and pulled out of the sack, same thing! This all happened at the beginning of December. We have our ideas as to why and why now. I'll not share those right now for they are just our opinions.

Don came to our house months after her passing in Connie's car (Juke). Burns was letting him in the garage. When Burns saw the Juke he smelled Connie; he was nowhere near the car!

Back to the Mother's Day 2016 part: I didn't mention because I didn't want to make Momma cry (any more), but I didn't have to, I looked up and noticed both momma and Burns acting just like me. They said about the same time: "I smell Connie, do ya'll?". Then we got our bill and just like the Father's Day incident (unusual) our bill was touched, cut in 1/2 this time. Momma and I smiled because that meant ours was free (the 2 mothers on Mother's Day).

Father's Day 2016 we took Daddy to Branson. I try to take them out of town on special days to get their minds on joyful things as much as I can. Each time, we're not met with sadness but joy. Praise! We had done things all day with no reminders of Connie. We left the amusement park later than planned and normally I would've said lets eat on the way and go on home since its so late. Strangely we not only ate inside, we ate at the place earlier everyone said they did not want to go! We went to Mel's Diner, the same place we went to on the anniversary of her passing (12/12/15). Well, here we sit and that all comes to mind, thinking well, why didn't we go on (I've got a long drive and I'm tired...).

Mel's has singing waitstaff. During Christmas we like going here because the waiters sing Christmas songs the whole time. We'd never been outside of Christmas. So, this night they were singing your typical "Branson tunes" not one gospel. We were almost finished when Connie came to my mind and it occurred to me that Father's Day was here and we had not had a touch from her. Jokingly I said in my mind, "Connie, you forgot." Momma had gone to the restroom, walking back she thought (she told me this later of course) the same thing I did at the same time! Neither one of us telling the other then. Then it happened: a waitress began singing the only Christian song sung of the night: "Uncloudy Day/The Unclouded Day". To you "youngsters" you may not even know that song. It is an old one for sure. One we don't sing anymore at our home church nor my church. Yet, this is the song the waitress chose. Why, I didn't catch at first. Even when she was singing it I didn't connect at all to Daddy. To Connie yes, the words are appropriate for where she is for sure. Me and Momma just sat there in that booth sobbing thinking of Connie. Yet to us, no connection with Daddy. While driving home I couldn't concentrate thinking of that song and what in the world connection did it have with Daddy because I knew it must due to the strangeness of the song itself being sung. Then it hit me like a ton of bricks (aka Connie). My memory became as clear on the details as if I was there again. When we were little, Daddy sang (bass) a "special" (a term you'll appreciate if you're a country churchgoer) once in a quartet at our church. They sang this! That is such a sweet memory and so like Connie. I can hear his voice so clearly as he bellowed out in that beautiful bass voice "Oh, they tell me"... . I could even see the other 3 men with with him, where he stood.. all of it. Connie always had a knack of coming up with the most thoughtful gifts, sometimes gifts that didn't cost anything. She labored over every gift to make sure it had a meaning for the recipient. This was one of those thoughtful gifts. "Thank you, Father!"

(Oh, they tell me of a home far beyond the skies

Oh, they tell me of a home far away

Oh, they tell me of a home where no storm clouds rise

Oh, they tell me of an unclouded day

Oh, the land of cloudless day

Oh, the land of an unclouded day

Oh, they tell me of a home where no storm clouds rise

Oh, they tell me of an unclouded day...)

Speaking of Daddy singing, Daddy has always sang in the choir at church. He hasn't been back up since Connie passed. We've never asked him why. Why not? I guess we just feel it's his private, sweet reason and too delicate a wound to touch with questions. I've often thought about it, although only to myself. Its nothing I've even asked Momma about. For me, I think the reason I haven't asked him or even Momma is because the reason I have deduced is self explanatory and needs no questioning. Let me explain: For as long as I can remember, I can see Daddy up there. He wasn't looking at the choir director or the people. He kept his eyes on me and Connie. I can remember it when we were little and still sitting with them. I can remember it when we grew up and were sitting with friends. I can remember it when we were older, sitting on the other side with our dates. I remember it in more recent years being there visiting with Momma and Daddy with my family.

As I mentioned many times, Connie always came in late. I always knew she was about to enter our pew because I'd see Daddy's face. He'd smile as if to say, "I see you, Shug"; that sweet, pleased smile. I recall my whole life seeing those loving eyes staring at us, that smile peeking through his singing. Knowing he'll not ever look out, in that venue at least, and see his "Big Shug" again. (FYI, I'm "Little Shug, Connie is "Big Shug" to Daddy. Neither Daddy or Momma call us by our given names).

Connie & Daddy

Just a couple more little additions that didn't really fit anywhere into the above: Connie had given me (before she passed) some clothes to sell on Ebay. There was a rain jacket. I don't know why but I checked the pockets. Connie didn't leave things in pockets; I don't either. Seems if you are in charge of the laundry, you've trained yourself not to (anyone that's had to get laundered paper off of clothes knows never to leave things in pockets). But in her pocket I found a business card for a hospital. It read: "Mercy" and had a cross on it. I found that when I was low for sure and seeing that word and that cross lifted me. A friend said even the word "Mercy"- "God truly gives mercy!" Of all business cards to have! To be more specific, this is the card from the hospital in Hot Springs where she passed away!

Sumo Japanese restaurant was where Momma and Connie ate last in Jonesboro. Connie had the waitress take their picture even. Momma saved the menu and even wrote their names by what they'd ordered. We've often commented on why Momma kept this menu. Why did Connie think to have their picture taken here? Going to Jonesboro wasn't monumental, why did they treat as such? God directed them too, that's why! It was later to be memorable as God knew because that was their last visit to Jonesboro. One day recently we (me and Momma) were talking about that very thing. Burns was playing his XBox. He said, "look!" One of the cars on the game of all things had a wrapped ad on for "SUMO Japanese Restaurant"!

My husband received a card from a online store. It came to his office addressed to: Connie Terry. Even when Connie lived in Conway (more than 8 years ago) she didn't use his office address of course and she wasn't "Terry" then! I wish I could post a picture of it on here. It looks almost like a sympathy card vs a store circular. On the front it says: "We remembered..." then it has a lady holding roses (the same color/kind roses as Don once gave Connie!). On the inside its marking Connie's "anniversary" it says of her first purchase with them. Her first purchase was her wedding outfit! And that wasn't a year ago, it was three! Why did they send this three years after! Its special to us, that's why!

Some of these things connected to her would be to an outsider not even worth mentioning. Perhaps some I did mention weren't even. Each to us has meant a great deal. Many to me are jaw dropping. Others just bring a smile to our face and a thankful whisper to the Lord. I can recall two "small touches": mailing in a broken glass for a replacement and the company sending the wrong color in exchange- they sent a purple one. Burns reaching in the cabinet to grab same glasses (brown), thinking of Connie at the time and although he grabbed the brown one, the purple one was in his hand. "Thank you, Father for each touch, they are all great and mighty to us".

On October 11,2015 we went on a trip. That is Connie's birthday. A strange thing happened at the hotel which made them reduce our hotel bill by 1/2.

On December 1, 2015 Momma hadn't seen her cardinals in the yard. On her way to the mailbox she said, "Connie, I haven't seen the cardinals today." In her mailbox was a *National Geographic* catalog and boom on the cover was a giant cardinal, nothing else.

September 2016, my best friend from high school treated me to a overnight stay in Memphis. This was way overdue for us and greatly needed for me. She felt like I needed this friend time and she was so right! "Thank you, Father!". As I'm about to explain, I wasn't the only one excited about it (and I don't mean my friend)...

My friend has for years had a sleeping disorder. She can't get to that REM sleep so therefore never dreams. She said the longest "dreams" if you can call them that her whole life seem like brief pictures, almost like scenes you see on TV as you change the channels quickly. The night before our sleepover she had an actual dream, her first! To me, this happening to her makes this all the more more miraculous. I'll quote:

"Cameron, last night I dreamed for the first time in my life (then she explained about her sleeping problem). It was about Connie! A car pulled up, Connie was in the passenger seat, no one was driving. She was wearing a black and white dotted blouse and was absolutely beautiful! There's something about the car too that's attached to my past with you but I just can't see what. Connie was beaming at me from ear to ear, as if to say, "Thank you, Cathy!"

We began talking about it, I wanted to get this car thing settled, but she wanted to keep talking about the way Connie looked and how she was so happy. I wondered if she was in the car she had with Don, her Juke. I asked and Cathy said "No, its an older car..." When she said "older" I thought, bingo, I've got it! I said, "Was it baby blue..." before I could go on she yelled, "Yes! It was YOUR car, the one you had in high school." We both started crying for many reasons. How appropriate that she be in *that* car. Of all things. That car was what was associated with Cathy and I. It was also Connie's first car. When she got a new one, it was handed down to me. This car was for years a topic of discussion for me and Connie, it held a ton of memories for us both.

Why the passenger seat, I'm still puzzled about. I can't explain how medicinal, if you will, this sleepover was for me. We talked non stop until almost dawn. When I say "we", I should say "me". I felt guilty the next day that I monopolized the time. Cathy said, "Nope, that was what this was for, you!" I have had such heartache since losing Connie and other monumental things along with that I can't go into. Connie knew I needed this desperately and God allowed her to thank

Cathy for giving me this. Imagine, a girl who had never dreamed...

"Thank you, sweet sister!" "Thank you, Father!"

When I got home, I texted Renee to tell her about it and mercy if she didn't recall the very blouse! She said it was one of her favorites. Momma used to sew and made most of our clothes. This was one she had made for Connie to wear at Easter, it had a matching skirt. Momma had stayed up all night (which she did often) so Connie could have Easter Sunday. Momma got a little gift from all of this too because Renee recalled how Connie bragged on that outfit that day (Easter) and how her momma had stayed up all night long just so she'd have a new outfit. Momma never knew that. When you're young sometimes we fail to tell our parents how much we appreciate

169

the things they sacrifice and do for us. It blessed Momma so I'm glad Cathy mentioned the blouse.

October 19 is Momma's birthday. She commented that usually in October/November her birds start to dwindle out since the fields in the area have been cut. This day, no birds EXCEPT for her red birds (2 this time). Connie never forgets!

December 12, 2016 (2nd anniversary of Connie's passing) we were in Branson again and eating at Mel's. Since Connie passed, we have never eaten here without a touch about Connie. There was a table full next to us. Momma always stares at other people's plates trying to see what they have. She always thinks "they" have something that looks good. She kept staring at this one lady's plate, never even noticing the lady. It was almost time to leave when she finally looked at the lady. Sure enough if she wasn't almost the spitting image of Connie! It was hard to look without crying so cried we did. Not only her face looked like Connie but her hairstyle, her hands and even the way she held her hands. Mercy if she didn't even wear glasses like Connie had. God is so faithful and so full of merciful gifts!

Chapter 17
Thank you, Lord

1 Corinthians 2:9 - "No eye has seen, no ear has heard, no mind has conceived what God has prepared for those who love Him." (NIV)

Like I said earlier, there are things that we've written down but

I didn't record here. It's one thing after another. Is this normal? I wish someone could answer that. I equate it not to normal, but miraculous. Not at all mysterious for we know the source of all miracles. In the last days (which is the time I believe at hand) there will be an increase in miracles both personal and global. In Mark 16 it says "signs will FOLLOW those who believe." When we look to the Lord and seek His Kingdom and His righteousness, signs and wonders will follow. It should never be the signs that we seek. Our God is the same God today as in Genesis 1. He is still a supernatural, loving God. In each case regarding the miracles we've been shown, we seek God first in our actions and expectations then He shows us these things. Many could argue that also in the last days Scripture speaks of the enemy gaining power and working signs and wonders. The Scripture says that (Matthew 24:24, 2 Thessalonians 2:9 and more) so yes, I believe that. The defense we have to protect against being deceived by that is staying in full fellowship with Christ and His Word and being able to distinguish between Christ's hand and voice versus the enemy's. We can speak and say, "According to the Word of God, I bind the devil's power to deceive me by pleading the Blood of Jesus. I will not let satan's forces operate. If this is You, Lord Jesus speaking to me, please say on."

John 10:5 - "And a stranger will they not follow, but will flee from him; for they know not the voice of strangers." (KJV)

John 10:27 - "My sheep hear my voice, and I know them, and they follow me." (KJV)

Very little time has passed in the scheme of things since Connie left, but in a way it seems like a lifetime. Much has changed in our lives as a family. Many heartaches and hardships have come and are still coming while I write. Many times we've yearned to talk to her, to get her advice. That's just one of the things we miss about her. Loss is so hard, I believe its the hardest thing people ever have to face. For my parents especially, losing a child is unlike losing any other relation. We think we have it hard when trials come but a loss puts it all into perspective. Renee sent me a quote recently, I loved what it said:

> *I believe the hardest part of healing after you've lost someone you love, is to recover the "you" that went away with them.*

Things that used to bother me don't seem to matter anymore. There has been good to come from losing Connie, in my opinion, our relationship with the Lord has strengthened, grown, and matured. If you would've asked me just a few years ago if I was close to the Lord I would've said yes, without hesitation. When I sit here and look back, that was not the case. Does it take a loss or a tragic event to bring us to our knees, often yes. Losing my only sibling so early in life, so unexpected was a jolt I was almost to weak to face. I can speak for my parents most assuredly. Many times it has almost been too much for them. Am I writing this to get pity? NO! I'm writing this for many reasons: to honor a sister who deserved it, to minister to someone else, to lead someone to the Lord, to in some way draw someone closer to the Lord, to be able to tell others what a caring, miracle performing, mighty, LIVING, loving God I serve. To be able to say I've been transported, to say God has remembered every occasion important to us, to say God has allowed us to be comforted by sight, sound, and smell is to just touch the surface. I've learned to not disregard testimonies of unexplained miracles as of I was once guilty. I am no longer a cynic. Reading this may not change your thoughts. Dare I admit it took me seeing a miracle face to face and to have me and my family literally transported to just name two, to change me.

We are all on a journey, a healing journey. One that will not end until we see Connie again face to face. We've all been privileged to see and hear her in our dreams, but long for it to be real. We are all healing and traveling through in our own way, all with the love of the Father's Hand and each other.

Recently Don wrote a letter to a friend who had lost their spouse as well at a young age. To me his letter was also a tool for his healing although his intention was to help his friend. Like I said earlier, sometimes we minister to ourselves without even knowing it by ministering to another. I wanted to include that letter in this story. After reading it I felt I had to include it. To me, it was a beautiful way for a loving husband to honor a deserving wife. And it may help someone else who is grieving. I'll only include a portion of the letter so as not to include parts relating to his friend's situation to protect her privacy, her heart. The letter reads as follows with some excerpts removed...

I felt the need to write you for some time but wasn't sure if I should...

I'm not going to ask how you're doing because I am quite certain even you aren't always sure these days and that only God knows. For me personally, it changes hourly. As I'm sure you've been told, I lost my wife almost a year before you lost... December 12, 2014. Although the circumstances were different, it was still an unexpected event that turned my world upside down. And now, a year and a half later I'm still asking God which way is up every morning and most nights. So I think I can say with some authority, that no one knows how you feel right now. Some of what we each are likely going through the other can relate to, but I'm pretty sure your grief is as unique to you as I feel mine is to me.

... And when friends comment "I noticed you're still wearing your wedding ring" as to subtly imply that it hurts your prospects for dating, you can tell them "the divorced remove their ring, the widowed don't". For me, I came to realize that ring was a symbol of Connie's love for me. Your ring is a promise that is just as valid today as it was the day he showed it to you and you said "YES" as well as the day you said "I do". You wear it as long and often as you want and you are entitled to. ...

175

You have experienced a loss- a loss as real and painful as losing an arm or leg, and truthfully, much more so. If you had lost an arm or leg, you would have numerous physical and emotional feelings, probably for a lifetime, and sometimes in ways that don't make sense. Many amputees report phantom pain for limbs that are no longer there- but the pain they feel is completely real.

My Dear Lady is gone from me and feelings associated with the grief are all over the map: hurt, guilt, remorse, relief (ouch), regret, loneliness, confusion, uncertainly, worry and a dictionary full of more words. Sometimes it burns, sometimes it's a stabbing pain, sometimes a dull ache, sometimes it's nauseating. It's so overwhelming its numbing.

And all of these feelings are real and don't let anyone tell you otherwise. Neither are any of them something to be ashamed of.

...

Some days I miss Connie. Some days I'm mad at Connie. Some days I laugh at Connie. Some days I laugh at myself because I know Connie would. And some days I am certain that I am laughing WITH Connie. Some days, all of the above 3-10 times over. Some days I am lonely in a room of 50 people. Some days I'm by myself and not lonely at all.

And it's real- every bit as real as her love for me. She really did love me in this life and loves me even now, just differently. ... I still talk to Connie. Thankfully she doesn't answer or I'd be checking into one of those places with padded rooms. But I talk to her on occasion. Sometimes when I'm regretting, I apologize. Sometimes when I'm mad I say Connie-Connie-Connie. Sometimes I tell her thank you for loving me. And in each case end up thanking God for bringing her into my life. I'm not asking or even wanting her to respond to me because she's moved on. She's graduated. She can love perfectly now and she has the perfect heart of Christ and because of Him can love me perfectly, along with everyone else that loved me in this life but has gone Home.

It's not fair. "Till death do us part" was supposed to be measured in decades and anniversaries named after precious metals. I promised to give Connie Crow's Feet -the wrinkles at the sides of the eyes that people that smile a lot get. We like to repeat the myth that marriage is forever. The truth is that it is a gift that is supposed to be for a short time we call "this life". But she was supposed to be mine longer than 1 year, 8 months and 14 days.

.... I can't say it will get easier. I can say I think you will get stronger- even on days that it seems you are just putting on a face while inside you are crying out to God "Father, I can't do this". Well He *is* your Father and when you can't, He WILL. There are days you need to come to the Throne Room of the Maker of the Universe and bow down and worship the Creator of All Existence. Then there are other times when you just need to be like a child and climb up into the lap of your Heavenly Father who built all of Time and Space just for you and let Him hold you. And lastly there are times you need to go for a walk with your best friend who sacrificed Himself for you. Every one of those is a perfectly valid way to look at your relationship with God and He wants to be all of them in your life when that's the God you need Him to be.

　　　　We don't know the details of God's plan for our lives, or the paths He will have us follow or the trials we will face. Some days I still wear my ring and others I don't. Whether I ever marry again, I have no clue and as sure as I say I won't, He'll cross my path with someone that I fall head over heels for. But if someone falls in love with the person I am now, they will have Connie to thank in part. She is a part of me just as my kids are a part of me and all the people who have sown and invested in my life. I am the person I am in large part because of Connie's impact on my life.

I encourage you to find a support group. I found my "grief support group" in a mixture of her sister (who is struggling with the loss of Connie), Connie's best friend (a remarried widow of one of my best friends from college), and a couple long term friends. They are people I can be totally honest with about my faults, how mad she could make me, how madly I loved her, how much she made me laugh, how good I feel today, how worn out I feel today, how the kids are, and how life is going. They can't understand how I feel but they can relate to it because each cared for Connie and each feels a loss. Together the best of Connie lives on.

Lastly, be who you need to be today. You will always be specific to someone... I'm always dad, uncle, I'm a computer geek, I'm Cameron's Brother (technically- in law but we decided to drop that), and so on. So decide who you need to be-...and if you need to just go somewhere and be quiet and anonymous, THAT'S OK TOO. I have 2 special places I don't go with anyone else so that I can just remember Connie. Not that I wouldn't go with others, but I intentionally go by myself.

To me, this letter could be written by anyone hurting, from any loss. I debated on whether or not to include but after praying about it and reading again I felt I should. It honors Connie as the loving wife, loving person she was but more than that I feel it could help someone. Grieving is hard. As I've said, grieving is a journey, a lifelong journey too. We need to help each other, we need to reach out. Doing that will not only help someone else but I feel it helps us too.

 I'm not talented enough to convey into words the impact these miracles/blessings have had on us, to convey in words what we saw, what happened to us. I do know God is active today, He's perhaps even showing His glory more intensely since time is drawing short. I believe we are to be as the Scripture says, "a light in the world". Keeping quiet about Connie's life, the events that have transpired since her passing would be to "hide under a bushel", I can't do that. Thank you, Lord for allowing us to experience this. Use us as your vessel to spread the word of your love, salvation, and awesome power! On June 10, 2015 Momma was looking in Connie's room. On her bedside table was a devotional book entitled: <u>Safe in the Arms of Jesus.</u> I think it is fitting to end the story on that. I have a feeling though God isn't finished.

Romans 8:18 - " For I consider that the sufferings of this present time are not worth comparing with the GLORY that is GOING to be revealed to us!" (HCS)

My final quote will be-

"Her absence is like the sky, spread over everything." -C. S.

Lewis

My last words will be-

to be continued...

Precious memories, too few - time that has passed like a mere vapor

"Nothing is ever really lost to us as long as we remember it." - LM Montgomery

"Every experience God gives us, every person He puts in our lives is the perfect preparation for a future that only He can see." ~ Corrie Ten Boom

Honoring Connie's Home-going- 1st anniversary

A sampling expression of Connie's love for the Lord in her own hand.

The year, 2001, I began reading this book in May, which put me through many a problems & temptations. But, as the book says – Only through absolute faith can we experience Gods unmatchless grace.

Thank you Lord, for giving me grace that I am so totally unworthly of, but I know how I received it and I thank you for it.

In Christ's Name

AMEN

A note to Momma and Daddy in her own hand. She had given this book to them on their 45th anniversary.

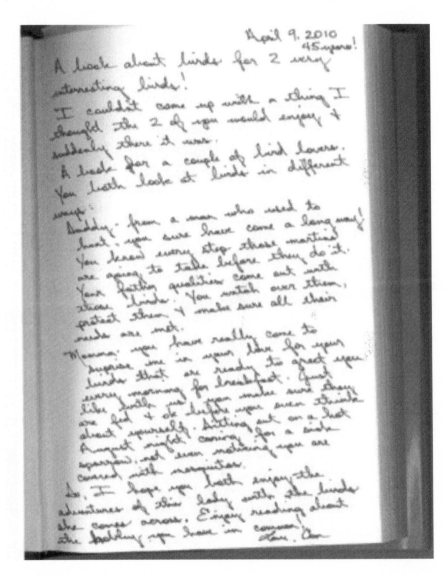

In loving memory of

Connie Hoggard Terry

October 11, 1966- December 12, 2014

beloved sister

Dr. Monty Clark

May 8, 1952- May 9, 2017

beloved husband

Made in the USA
Lexington, KY
04 May 2019